D0425903

THE SHIFT

THE SHIFT

The Transformation of Today's Marketers into Tomorrow's Growth Leaders

Scott M. Davis

Foreword by Philip Kotler

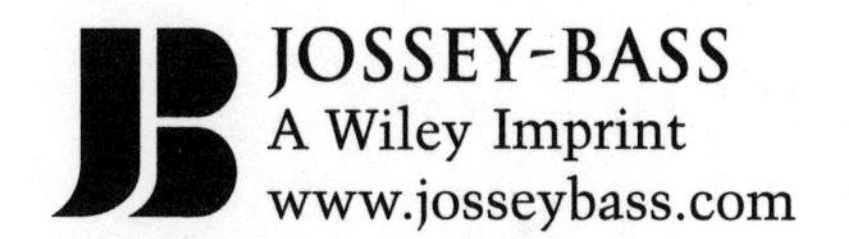

JOSSEY-BASS
A Wiley Imprint
www.josseybass.com

Published by Jossey-Bass
A Wiley Imprint
989 Market Street, San Francisco, CA 94103-1741—www.josseybass.com

Jossey-Bass books and products are available through most bookstores. To contact Jossey-Bass directly call our Customer Care Department within the U.S. at 800-956-7739, outside the U.S. at 317-572-3986, or fax 317-572-4002.

Jossey-Bass also publishes its books in a variety of electronic formats. Some content that appears in print may not be available in electronic books.

Cataloging-in-Publication data on file with the Library of Congress.

ISBN: 978-0470-38838-9

Printed in the United States of America
FIRST EDITION
HB Printing 10 9 8 7 6 5 4 3 2 1

CONTENTS

FOREWORD

For many years, I have been making a strong argument in my meetings with top executives that marketing has to take on a stronger role within their organizations. Marketing is more than a function that supports sales and creates communications materials, and it has considerably more to offer in helping to shape where a company is going and reach its growth aspirations. I believe that marketers have the ability to partner with the CEO and other executives in ways that most companies have not experienced. To this point, I also believe that today's marketers must be charged with helping their company create a future portfolio of offerings, prices, services, experiences, messages, and media to win over customers and capture a growing share of a customer's wallet and loyalty, and not just his or her awareness. However, this premise does raise some questions.

First, is marketing equipped to take on a higher-profile role? I believe the answer could be yes, but today many companies, by default, are hiring marketers for stereotypical roles, usually encompassing managing just the promotional P of the 4 P's (product, price, place, and promotion). How could a marketer hired primarily for promotional skills and experiences truly have the ability to become a growth driver within the organization? To succeed in a more strategic role, these marketers would have to obtain the right levels of training, cross-company internal support, and executive-level trust in taking on higher-level and broader responsibilities, or the company will have to go outside to recruit the talent required. Ultimately CEOs and boards must determine whether they are going to make an internal or external investment in marketing to truly pay off the role within their organizations.

The good news is that I am starting to see some companies take a more expansive view of marketing by starting to hire heads of marketing, or CMOs, who have a much greater ability to manage and influence others. These marketers are termed Visionary Marketers in *The Shift*, which is appropriate on two fronts. First, they have a more expansive vision of what their company is trying to achieve in the longer term and what role marketing can play in helping their company achieve its sales and profit growth objectives. Second, the term *visionary* is appropriate for this reimagined role, as it foreshadows what the future profile of successful marketers should encompass.

Another major question is whether CEOs and their senior executive team will expand their ideas of what marketing can accomplish. CEOs tend to see marketing as a department that comes into play after the product has been made, and thus their primary job is to help sell the product or service. I would argue instead that marketing must be seen as having a key role in, and responsibility for, setting the strategic direction for the firm. Management guru Peter Drucker said it best over thirty years ago: "A company has only two basic functions: innovation and marketing." I believe this still to be true, and thus marketing has to truly become a strategic asset so companies can extract the full value out of this important function.

So, can company officers beyond the CEO alter their perceptions of the value that excellent marketing can deliver to the organization, or will they continue to keep marketing boxed in narrowly? The answer depends on four variables that Scott Davis discusses: the profile of the CEO and the board, the industry that the company competes in, the experience the company has had with marketing as an asset, and the skills of individual marketers. Whether a marketer ends up being more of a Tactician Marketer or truly a Visionary Marketer is housed within an algorithm resulting from these four variables.

At the end of the day, as Davis contends, the marketers who will stand out will own some combination of the following attributes. They will operate with a P&L mind-set, they will have an accountability and impact orientation, they will have a seat at the C-table, and they will constantly be looking to help their company orient itself around the Five Shifts encompassed within this book.

I am a big believer that marketing, when operating at its very best, should own the following areas of responsibility: opportunity identification, new product development, customer attraction, customer retention and loyalty building, and order fulfillment. A company that truly believes that marketing should be charged with these five responsibility areas has already philosophically made *The Shift*. For these companies, this book will help them execute against that philosophy. For the vast majority of other companies that have not yet begun, *The Shift* is a must-read to help marketers and their respective organizations move ahead and thrive.

Philip Kotler
S. C. Johnson and Son Distinguished Professor
of International Marketing
Kellogg School of Management
Northwestern University

To Ethan, Benjamin, and Emma—always remember to dream big and keep your hearts and minds open to life's possibilities. I love you more than you will ever know.

ACKNOWLEDGMENTS

The Shift is the combined efforts and ideas of many people I have had the honor of working with over the years. My past and current client experiences and relationships have helped shape the premise of this book, and so I thank the dozens of marketing and business leaders who agreed to be interviewed for this book. Their business experiences, wisdom, and leadership approaches helped substantiate and put texture behind the very concept of the Visionary Marketer.

These individuals are: Paul Ballew (Nationwide), Jim Blann (American Express), Sean Burke (GE Healthcare), Pam Butcher (Dow), Dennis Cary (United Airlines), Ranjana Clark (Wells-Fargo), Randall Clouser (Zurich Financial), Beth Comstock (GE), Gary Elliott (HP), Tulin Erdem (NYU–Stern School of Business), Rory Finlay (Jim Beam), Carter Franke (JP Morgan Chase), Mark Gambill (CDW), Chris Gibson (UnitedHealthcare), Shira Goodman (Staples), Carolyn Groobey (eBay), Bob Harris (Lending

Tree), Tony Hsieh (Zappos), Claire Huang (Fidelity), Barry Judge (Best Buy), Yvonne La Penotiere (Carlson Hotels), Ann Lewnes (Adobe), Oliver Loch (UBS), Damian Lucas (Cemex), Martina Ludescher (DKSH), Suzanne McCarron (ExxonMobil), Steve Meyer (Dell Services), John Nottingham (Nottingham-Spirk), Tom O'Toole (Hyatt), Steve Pacheco (FedEx), Stephen Quinn (Walmart), Becky Saeger (Charles Schwab), Nabil Shabshab (JohnsonDiversey), Andy Stefanovich (PLAY), Adam Stotsky (NBC Universal), Brian Swette (Burger King), Tracy Tuten-Ryan (Virginia Commonwealth University), and Mark Waller (NFL).

I owe enormous thanks to all of the chapter co-owners and colleagues who helped shape and write the chapters in *The Shift*. Their expertise and insights have greatly contributed to each of the chapters and provided detailed arguments and logic. Their incredible thought leadership, hard work, and dedication made this book possible. They pushed my thinking in new directions and through that enhanced our firm's thinking as we continue addressing new challenges and opportunities in the broad marketing arena. With that, my thanks and professional admiration go out to Mitch Duckler, Andy Flynn, Jay Milliken, Brian Myers, Chiaki Nishino, Andy Pierce, Jeff Smith, and Jill Steele.

I cannot thank Cindy Levine and Tina Cicci enough for being my "partners-in-crime" in pulling the pieces together into a coherent book. They helped frame the book early on, helped me through all of the interviews and data collection, reviewed and critiqued chapter outlines and full chapters, and hit the Reply button at all times of the day and night. I could not have completed this book without their help, and I truly appreciate our friendship and relationship over our many years together.

The hundreds of hours of time that went into this book would never have been completed without all the help that I received from others within Prophet. Specifically, I thank Jill Steele, Amanda Nizzere, and Karen Woon for all of my requests for copies of studies and surveys. Thanks to Tobias Ammann, Selim Aykut,

Melissa Esmundo, Andrea Hilber, and Mark Schulman for their time researching companies, building case studies, and editing the book. Thank-you to Joann Guidici for helping with the approval process in all quotations used throughout the book.

Special thanks go out to Tracy Riordan, who helped me manage my book writing time from the day we began until we sent off the final manuscript. I very much appreciate her logistical support for all the interviews conducted and meetings scheduled, as well as her patience to roll with me on this, even though it was against her instinct of totally being in control.

I thank the Senior Partners at Prophet for their support: Michael Dunn, Mike Leiser, Andy Pierce, Kevin O'Donnell, and Simon Marlow. In addition, I would like to thank Andrea Ivey Harris. Thanks to all of them for honoring my book writing times and helping with the extra work that I put on their shoulders. This is an enormous effort, and I could not have completed it without their support. I hope we have all collectively benefited from the effort.

An additional round of thank-yous to my friends David Aaker, for continuing to inspire me; Mark Leiter, for continuing to push me to write the best book I could; and Carl Bochmann, for continuing to push me to get this book off the ground.

Thank-you to the Association of National Advertisers for our long-standing and productive partnership and, in particular, to Michael Palmer for being an incredible friend and partner over our nine-year relationship.

To Phil Kotler: thank you for continuing to pioneer and push the marketing dialogue to new and exciting places and for writing such a highly relevant Foreword for *The Shift*—the Kellogg connections continue to amaze me over the years.

I give a special thank-you to Kathe Sweeney and the rest of the team at Jossey-Bass. As with my previous books, I could not imagine a better publishing partner, and I truly treasure our relationship that has extended over more than ten years. I look forward to another decade of partnering together.

And finally I am grateful to my family. To Larry and Sandy: thank-you for always being there for us. To my mom and dad: I could not ask for two better friends and people in my life. They continue to teach me how to live my life in fuller and richer ways every day. To my wife Debbie, who again shouldered the burden on the home front of writing this book. I could not have done this without her love and support. And to my children, Ethan, Benjamin, and Emma, who continue to light up my life in ways that are unimaginable to them, I love you. I love them more than they could ever know.

May 2009 Scott M. Davis
Glencoe, Illinois

PREFACE

It's All About Growth

Successful marketing executives today aren't acting quite like marketers of the past. Welcome to a new era in Marketing, an era in which Visionary Marketers know:

No one is better suited to drive the growth agenda than the head of Marketing.

Yes—*growth*. These Visionary Marketers are seizing the challenge to become the senior executive in charge of their company's growth agenda. Clearly this is a golden moment in time for all marketers to rewrite the traditional playbook and shift their responsibilities from supporting sales to direct line responsibility for successful and profitable growth.

This new breed has guts. They represent a dramatic shift from traditional marketers, who are often limited to running the agency relationship, supporting the sales force, and constantly being squeezed for the nickels they do not have. These traditional marketers live in a short-term world, built on a narrow (and narrowing) platform of marketing communications and promotions.

Dozens of Visionary Marketers have seized the moment: they know that marketing, at its very best, holds the keys to growth. From deeply understanding today's and tomorrow's customers' needs, wants, behaviors, and media consumption patterns, to translating these into new products, services, experiences, and relationships that customers want, these Visionary Marketers are helping their organizations match these customer dynamics with internal capabilities for maximum external impact.

These Visionary Marketers have made *The Shift*, and they have a compelling argument to make. Listen to four of them:

- Russ Klein, marketing leader of Burger King Corporation, has the guts to assert, "Anything that's a growth factor is fair game for me to stick my nose into." Klein is responsible for product mix, pricing strategy, product development, market planning, supply chain, and mix management, in addition to more traditional marketing responsibilities. Everyone in the company considers Klein to be the CEO's right-hand man, as reflected in his title—President, Global Marketing Strategy and Innovation.
- Stephen Quinn, Chief Marketing Officer (CMO) at Walmart, continues to shed light on how the world's largest retailer can grow organically. Using robust insights, Quinn has helped focus the organization on the segments that matter—those that are open to Walmart's proposition and can provide growth and healthy margins. Quinn states that "even though most of America shops at Walmart, not all of America is Walmart's target." Walmart sales are climbing ahead of those of its competitors.

- At GE, marketing, led by Beth Comstock, has embraced the CEO's charter to be a GE growth catalyst. Marketing co-owns growth and innovation because CEO Jeff Immelt believes in the link between customer insights and growth. Immelt made Marketing responsible for owning customer insights, and, as a result, the growth agenda of one of the world's most successful companies.
- Barry Judge, CMO of Best Buy, talks with the board not about a "new ad campaign" but about the "consumer demand landscape and how to drive share through driving [consumer] preferences." He seized the moment when other executives "were having trouble generating growth using the customer as the lens. Marketing brought the insight, the framework, and the judgment to operationalize the customer centric-strategy for growth."

Five Aspects of *The Shift*

This book expands on the stories of these Visionary Marketers, and others like them, who have become empowered as executives with responsibility for growth and results. From them and other sources of insight, this book distills what's going on, how and why marketers are succeeding, and how you too can make and maintain this shift. This book sets out five shifts for marketers to make to become Visionary Marketers:

- A shift from creating marketing strategies to driving business impact
- A shift from controlling the message to galvanizing your network
- A shift from incremental improvements to pervasive innovation
- A shift from managing marketing invesments to inspiring marketing excellence

- A shift from an operational focus to a relentless customer focus

Why Should I Change? I'm Okay

Most marketers will not have a choice: they must make *The Shift*. Look at the facts: shortening of CMO tenure, backlash from everyone, greater calls for accountability, and a growing divide among Marketing, Sales, and Finance all point to the need for a fundamental change in the formula for a successful marketing operation. Numerous industry studies and reports, interviews with over thirty global CMOs and CEOs, and case studies drawn from these interviews and our professional experiences have also made this clear.

With trends like these, time is running out for traditional marketers. Bill McDonald, Executive Vice President of Brand Management at Capital One, states, "When Marketing takes on a life of its own and CMOs worship at the altar of creative or cool Internet strategies, they risk being misaligned with what their colleagues [want from] the function: greater responsibility for growth."

Visionary Marketers know that there are new rules for success: drive insights into the organization, help identify and drive forward new opportunities, and help execute them flawlessly in the marketplace. Visionary Marketers have no issue with taking the risk of operating in a directionally correct manner when launching new initiatives, products, retail formats, and programs. They know that having a high-confidence 60%-plus answer, similar to Burger King Corporation's rule of operation, works just fine, and they can gain an incredible competitive advantage over those who continue to operate at only 100% levels of confidence before they can make a move.

Many marketers acknowledge *The Shift* and have recognized the need to go beyond insights and innovation to execution that delivers impact. JohnsonDiversey SVP and CMO Nabil Shabshab puts it this way: "We have decided to make the expedition to

Mt. Everest. We have all of the right equipment. . . . We are finally at the base. . . . We can actually see the peak . . . but getting there is an intricate act that requires focus, resilience, and very well coordinated execution by all members of the climbing party."

Shabshab knows that at the Board and CEO levels, demands for business results are acute and stringent, with far-reaching implications. In some cases, the focus has moved beyond revenue and share growth and is now on return on investment or invested capital and shareholder value. As the stakes keep getting higher for all executives, it is only right that the spotlight shines intensely on Marketing and its ability to contribute to shareholder value in a significant manner.

New Marketing Truths About Marketing Success

CEOs and Boards are demanding that Marketing become a strategic growth driver and catalyst for profitable growth. To meet that demand, Marketing must make certain that its insights pervade the organization, thereby helping the company drive its growth agenda and reach its financial goals and aspirations. To meet these demands, the Visionary Marketer must learn these new truths about what Marketing must do to succeed in the future:

- Drive strategic, board-level discussions on growth.
- Own balanced short- and long-term perspectives, always focusing on in-market, profitable impact.
- Recognize that customers own the brand, and be responsible (along with the rest of the organization) for guiding and enhancing brand growth through a growing network of influence.
- Drive profitable, insight-driven strategic initiatives and innovations through an organization-wide innovation ecosystem.

- Co-own the broad-based customer acquisition budget with the rest of the executive team.
- Lead by executing in a directionally correct manner, optimizing through a continuous test, learn, and adapt model.
- Work in a cross-functional, collaborative way with other functional areas (Sales, Finance, Information Technology, and Human Resources), revolving around the customer.

Table P.1 shows how the five broad shifts of this book correspond with these new marketing truths. It also reflects the older mind-set that is yielding to these changes. Subsequent chapters of this book tackle each of the shifts.

Table P.1 New Marketing Truths

Five Shifts	The Old Mind-Set	New Marketing Truths
First Shift: From creating marketing strategies to driving business impact	Marketing provides inputs for the growth agenda Marketing has a short-term mind-set and drives toward execution	Marketing drives strategic, board-level discussions on growth Marketing owns balanced short- and long-term perspectives, always focusing on in-market, profitable impact
Second Shift: From controlling the message to galvanzing your network	Marketing owns and controls the brand	Customers own the brand Marketing, along with the rest of the organization, is responsible for guiding and enhancing brand growth through its growing network of influence

Third Shift: From incremental improvements to pervasive innovation	Marketing drives insights and new product efforts	Marketing drives profitable, insight-driven strategic initiatives and innovations through an organization-wide innovation ecosystem
Fourth Shift: From managing marketing investments to inspiring marketing excellence	Marketing owns the marketing communications budget Marketing looks for a 100% correct answer	Marketing co-owns the broad-based customer acquisition budget with the rest of the executive team Marketing leads by executing in a directionally correct manner, optimizing through a continuous test, learn, and adapt model
Fifth Shift: From an operational focus to a relentless customer focus	Marketing is a functional area, often operating in a silo Organizations overemphasize optimizing efficiency, versus customer needs	Marketing works in a cross-functional, collaborative influence-based way with other functional areas, revolving around the customer

Sounds Too Risky?

Perhaps you feel secure right now and don't see the need to make these shifts. *Why*, you ask, *would I need to start acting like other executives who run a business unit, with direct profit and loss responsibility?* Certainly, taking on executive responsibility for revenue growth is risky. Of course, you could bank on the "Why should we?" inertia currently in place in many organizations to continue.

But sooner or later, your CEO will want to change the way your company battles for the hearts and minds of the customer. Why? Because sooner or later your CEO will face a confluence of changes and challenges. These challenges will range from the overcommoditization of everything and the resulting lack of differentiation to the proliferation and fragmentation of messaging. All of this occurs within a competitive environment that sees action and competitive reaction happening at a breakneck pace. Factor in the increasingly global, chilly economy, which is always dynamic and rarely dependable and one can see why the war for the customer dollar feels like such a battle.

This confluence of changes and challenges, and thus apparent lack of control, seems, well, out of control. That is why many of your fellow marketers will hesitate to make changes, but your CEO won't. He or she will realize that the business must transform how it operates and competes so that it wins. The CEO will look within the business for help in meeting these challenges—perhaps to Marketing, but perhaps to other functions as well. If you don't step up to the challenge, then Marketing and your role will be pushed further into the traditional marketing paradigm.

The bottom line is that you cannot avoid the changes taking place in the marketing landscape. They are permanent, and you need to figure out how to adapt. *The Shift* showcases how to adapt to this new marketing landscape and how you can take steps forward to become a successful catalyst for growth within your company. To make the argument for change within your company, and in particular, marketing, ask your CEO, "Who owns the intersection between capturing customers and capturing profitable growth? Who will see these intersecting challenges as one and the same? Who can drive and co-own the growth agenda, along with the CEO?" The answer is not always clear.

Building the Case for the Marketer as Growth Champion and Catalyst

Each of the Visionary Marketers interviewed for this book thought hard before making the plunge into growth, but none of them is sorry that he or she did. Becky Saeger, CMO of Charles Schwab, admitted that she pushed ahead because she knew there was no other way: "I had to establish myself as a partner on the management team to the CEO, COO, and CFO and build credibility as a business partner. Now the other members of the team know I'm one of them. I'm on this management team to run and grow the business." Now is the time to do what Saeger did: prove to your CEO that Marketing must become an integral part of the executive team and the growth agenda.

Forward-thinking CEOs are asking Marketing to join them on the journey to growth. Thus, you need to join the ranks of the Visionary Marketers who are already leading the charge to growth in their organizations by devising new and better ways to win new customers, while building deeper and more meaningful relationships with current customers, all in the service of erecting an impenetrable, competitor-proof wall.

To help your CEO see the importance of this, tell the stories about marketers like Klein, Quinn, Saeger, Comstock, and Judge. They learned that by helping to determine how to protect, defend, and develop the core customer base while finding and securing new and profitable customer segments, they have the tools to sell the other senior executives that Marketing can and should have a permanent seat at the senior executive table. No one other than Marketing is better equipped to aggregate and integrate all insights, lead the dialogue around breakthrough or white space opportunities, and coordinate, organize, and inspire all of the functions and business units across the enterprise to execute profitably and flawlessly.

The Visionary Marketers mentioned in this book are driving the growth agenda alongside the CEO, CFO, COO, and others on the executive team. Based on customer insights, Visionary Marketers will ask and answer the tough questions tied to knowing which customers to delight, which customers to just serve, and, importantly, which customers to fire. They will also be able to address, with facts, the challenge that most companies are wrestling with of acquired versus organic customer growth. They will be catalysts for driving the right conversations, debates, and decisions to get to the best growth outcome. And they will be astute enough to know they need enterprise-wide support—whether it is additional resources, capabilities, coalitions, or time—to walk the walk successfully.

The Time Is Now

Your opportunity for *The Shift* is near. Your company needs your help in its quest to drive the double-digit growth and returns that analysts, stakeholders, and investors expect to see again. Visionary Marketers may even see the signals before their CEOs do and will fight back with words and actions tied to insights, inspiration, innovation, execution, accountability, and impact. As Saeger tells it, "Schwab did lose its way after the dot.com bust. I could see that no one could find a new answer. That's when I decided if I didn't step up, no one would."

The days of marketing strategies and business strategies being created primarily independent of one another and in different documents, with different authors, and written in different fonts is going to end. The best marketers are creating integrated perspectives that start with the growth aspirations of the organization.

The best organizations will absorb a new philosophy about Marketing and its role. Listen to the argument that Burger King's former Chairman, Brian Swette, made to the board in asserting the importance of Marketing to Burger King's future. Swette stressed to the board his three-part belief in the power of Marketing: "First, Marketing has to be the brand champion. Second, Marketing has the most intense and direct understanding of the core customer and should leverage and share those insights with every pocket of the organization. Third, and most important, Marketing can and should effectively act as the center of growth—in terms of both our current portfolio of products as well as in driving new products in the future." Swette knew that CEO John Chidsey was looking for a go-to person in crafting and executing the growth agenda. CMO Russ Klein has met and exceeded expectations for this role.

Of course, few companies are as farsighted as Burger King in having an explicit growth champion or catalyst on its executive team, who acts as a partner to the CEO, in articulating and achieving the growth agenda. Although many marketers own aspects of the growth agenda, few have the integrated perspective across the organization that most CEOs desire.

Thus, through the confluence of necessity and opportunity, there has never been a better time for both the organization as a whole and marketers as individuals to step up and make the right shifts not only to survive, but to capitalize and ultimately thrive in their respective markets and organizations.

The time is now. Let's start to make *The Shift*!

INTRODUCTION

Preparing to Make *The Shift*

Do you recall any of these *Advertising Age* headlines from the past few years?

"CMO Leaving Home Depot."

"CMO Leaving Microsoft."

"CMO Leaving Chrysler."

"Wendy's Changing CMO again."

"Domino's CMO Leaving."

"Dow Jones CMO Resigns."

What was your first clue that marketing priorities were shifting? Maybe it was the astonishing number of op-ed pieces, articles, discussion panels, and features written about the phenomenon; the pace reminds you of the Breaking News scroller at the bottom of

CNN's nightly news. You might think Spencer Stuart should publish its survey tracking the average CMO's tenure not just annually but as a weekly box score within the business section.

Is your first reaction to these many notices, *How do I save my job?* Good question. Here's the answer. You need to be more accountable while doing more with less. You need to actively collaborate with your peers and stop acting so independently. You also need to engage strategically as well as creatively. And all of that needs to happen within a culture that continues to remind you to do your day job while providing space to try something new.

Voices from the Front Line

Unfortunately, many CEOs and CMOs have historically placed Marketing in a small box with a narrow set of responsibilities. As a result, a circular mentality continues to dominate most executive perceptions about what Marketing is doing versus what it should be doing. But why does that circle go unbroken? If you listen to some of the conversations that CEOs are having with heads of marketing on a daily basis, you can better understand why this circular mentality exists:

"What font size are you using in our catalogue? And why is the font of our phone number a smaller size than the rest of the text?"

"I just gave the go-ahead for Sales to hire its own agency. Not a problem, right?"

"You lost the battle when you started talking about changing our logo."

"There's nothing wrong with Asia-Pacific naming everything [every product, service, feature, benefit]. Doesn't hurt our effort. Stick to your job."

"Don't talk to me about segmentation! You know that more feet on the street trumps some fancy segments with names like 'price shoppers' or 'value seekers.' "

> "I want your report tonight using customer stats to tell me whether it costs more to keep the old customer or buy a new one."
>
> "Listen, I saw another journal report about the effectiveness of catalogues and direct mail versus your so-called website click conversion rates. So get off it, and write the damn letters."
>
> "Where is our Facebook page?"

Why do all of these conversations feel so tactical in nature? Why do executive teams stick to deeply engrained opinions about marketing's role and its overall readiness to become a strategic asset? Why don't all CEOs see the need to make a shift?

The Reason Most CEOs (Including Yours) Don't Shift

Many companies and their CEOs continue to operate in a time warp when it comes to the value that Marketing can bring to the organization. The reality is that some of this devaluation is self-inflicted. Adam Stotsky, former SVP of Marketing of the Sci-Fi Channel and current President of Marketing for NBC Entertainment, concurs: "Far too many CMOs come to the role with only knowledge about communications and advertising." Becky Saeger, CMO of Schwab, admits, "If you are on the team as just a traditional marketer, then you will never be viewed as a critical strategic player. You have to plug yourself in as a person running a business."

To be fair, many marketers complain they cannot shift into a strategic growth mode because they're buried under the overwhelming amount of work they're supposed to accomplish. Many say they have enough time only to remain in the control tower directing traffic—time for some strategic efforts, but mostly tactical. And when they do attempt to offer strategic opinions, they are not always effective. Steve Meyer, whose head of marketing roles have included Dell Services and Trilogy Software, says, "We've all been in meetings where traditional 'marketing experts' try to make a key point and eyes roll because there's not much depth or operating insight."

In a corollary to this problem, the strategy of many marketing executives to advance their careers by owning the concept of brand has begun to backfire. Too often, CEOs misunderstand the word *brand* as a logo or tagline. In other words, CEOs think brands are all about marketing communications. To put it another way, Marketing is doing a terrible job of marketing itself.

Similarly, there has been some misalignment between corporate and business unit marketing, which causes confusion, distrust, and budget battles that corporate marketing rarely wins, reinforcing internal negative perceptions. If the two marketing groups can't align, how is the rest of the organization supposed to view them as having strategic perspective?

This internal marketing difficulty often pales in comparison with the great divide that still exists between Marketing and Sales in many companies. Steve Meyer puts it this way: "Every company wrestles with the Sales and Marketing divide at some level. It's universal. No matter what organizational structure you have, you have to bridge that gap." Beth Comstock, CMO of GE, agrees: "There will always be tension between the two groups, although time, clarity in roles, and over-communication helps to ease that tension."

Russ Klein at Burger King Corporation adds, "I appreciate the dynamic that 'this may be an engineering- or a sales-driven company' with Sales as the alpha dog, but the marketing professional can't accept that as a reason not to roll up his sleeves and change the dialogue!"

If CEOs Do Not Want to Shift, How Can We?

Of course, a shift is difficult to do, and it doesn't happen overnight. But marketers like Klein and Meyer manage to do two important and successful things to get out of these traditional traps and seize the growth agenda. First, they shift marketing's profile, as a function and as individuals, to a more strategic one. Once the profile shifts and Marketing becomes a key strategic driver of the growth agenda, it becomes easier to be the strategic partner to the CEO and an undeniable asset to the organization.

The new formula for success starts with a new imperative. Marketers must become deeper strategic thinkers and bring that capability to bear across more of the business landscape. Those who contribute strategically and use their skills, capabilities, and knowledge will accomplish both shifts. That's the path Mark Waller, Senior Vice President of Marketing and Sales of the National Football League, has been taking.

His responsibilities build on each other: "First, I'm charged with having absolute clarity of consumer understanding. Second, I must translate that understanding into brand and business building strategies, and finally, I have to have a plan to commercialize those strategies in the market."

Waller's on to an approach that can be leveraged for you to become the guru of growth in your company. Visionary Marketers who have made *The Shift* agree that there really is only one purpose in making a shift: to help drive the company's growth goals and agenda—in effect, becoming the CEO's partner.

Visionary Marketers' Recipe for Success

The marketer who aspires to become the CEO's true partner in growth needs to bring together a balance of hard and soft skills. Think of this as akin to a recipe at a five-star restaurant where the chef carefully blends ingredients. The aspiring Visionary Marketer must:

- Consistently exceed expectations for marketing excellence.
- Build operating credibility with the CEO, CFO, and the rest of the C-suite.

- Show capability and muscle in driving strategic discussions at the corporate level.
- Consistently innovate across the enterprise.
- Lead by example, and inspire the organization to deliver results based on world-class marketing and business strategies and plans.

Of course, the basic ingredient—exceeding your company's expectations for marketing excellence—is a prerequisite to earning the right for a more strategic profile. If you can't handle the responsibilities you already have, then why should the CEO think you're ready for more? That's the stark, realistic situation at the top—CEOs will bring the right marketer into the inner circle, but that marketer must be proven. By successfully executing a world-class marketing plan, intimately tied to the company's strategic growth plan, and delivering quantifiable results, you will make a convincing argument that you as a marketer can play two roles simultaneously: that of a great strategic thinker and that of a great in-market executor.

Stephen Quinn, CMO of Walmart, admits that early in his tenure as CMO, he did everything, big and small, with a purpose. If he needed to write the weekly circular, he had no issue with doing the task himself. Although he had aspirations for the role that went far beyond the circular, he also knew that he would be judged as much on executing in a manner that would delight the 1.5 million store associates and 140 million weekly shoppers as he would be on thinking strategically.

Some CMOs with successful backgrounds as operators or business strategists are accountable beyond delivering on their marketing communication goals. Meyer, for example, believes "there's no substitute for putting real points on the board—led by analytics focused on true business impact rather than just traditional brand metrics like advertising tracking and equity studies. You can earn a real seat at the table."

Move from the Expected to the Unexpected—From Tactician to Visionary Marketer

Fully embracing *The Shift* helps to take the marketer's role from Tactician to Facilitator to Leader to Visionary (Figure I.1). Each role has specific attributes, and each allows marketers to see, much like a great brand identity is earned over time, that they can follow an aspirational path, earning their way to the leadership position they know they should possess.

As Tactician, the marketer is responsible for succeeding at delivering on a set of tactics or programs required to fulfill a strategic imperative. The Tactician, in effect, operates with a checklist or a to-do list of activities to achieve over a calendar year, and their value is often measured by the amount of "stuff" checked off. The Tactician tends to stay in the traditional marketing box, playing the functional role well, but is not viewed as an important or critical asset across the organization.

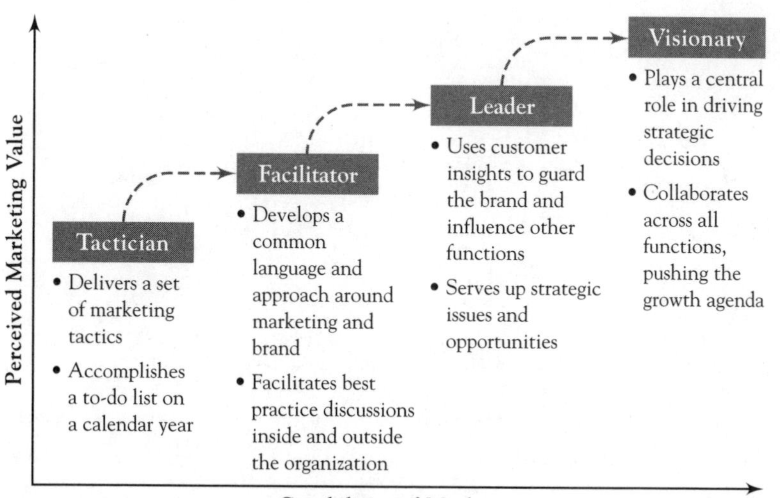

Figure I.1 The Evolution of the Marketer's Role

The Facilitator incorporates all of the Tactician responsibilities while also beginning to help the organization as a whole develop and leverage shared approaches to traditional marketing communications and sales. This role develops a common language around marketing and brand and develops approaches, tools, and methodologies. The Facilitator starts to lead discussions around best practices inside and outside the organization. Although Facilitators are not usually viewed as strategically as their peers, they are starting to play on a broader platform and building a voice within the organization.

The Leader carries out all of the Tactician and Facilitator responsibilities and uses customer insights and knowledge, beginning to show Marketing's customer-led strategic muscle throughout the organization. The Leader is known as the guardian of the brand, the keeper of the customer, a savvy marketing return-on-investment investor. The Leader lives up to this title primarily within Marketing, while recognizing the need to become more influential with other functions, such as Human Resources, Finance, Operations, and Sales. Although not always expected, the Leader looks to serve up strategic issues, opportunities, and dialogues across the organization, and drive toward customer-insight-led opportunities (in the broadest sense of the word) that can move the whole organization forward.

The Visionary Marketer encompasses all of these other roles and also plays that central role in driving strategy—from eliciting imperatives to tiering them, prioritizing them, and putting economic values around each. In addition, the Visionary Marketer proactively collaborates across all functions, consistently pushes the growth agenda, has deeply seeded relationships with the CEO and the Board, and is always commercially oriented.

Ultimate success comes from recognizing the importance of achieving each aspect of each type of marketing role, as well as recognizing that each role builds on successful achievement of the responsibilities housed in the previous one. You need to accumulate, and perhaps disperse or delegate responsibilities within each role to others.

Take Yourself and Your Company into Account

To a large degree, the ability to shift from Tactician to Visionary Marketer depends on your company's point of view on Marketing and the level of strength, influence, power, experience, and skill that the marketer demonstrates. In fact, a real debate is underway about whether it is the company or the marketer who has to make *The Shift*. But it may be that the debate is over, because, without a doubt, it is both.

Consider the following composite job description from a variety of CMO searches for Fortune 500 companies:

> **Strategic Growth-Oriented Marketing Executive**
>
> Board seeks new role for high-growth, global organization. Individual needs to focus on profitable growth and customer acquisition, be the brand champion, have the ability to manage between and across all 4 P's while collaborating with the executive team. We are looking for someone with operating credibility, someone adept enough to incorporate a P&L mind-set into every decision he or she makes. Impact, influence, and accountability will be hallmarks of success for this newly created position.

Traditionally companies looking for this type of marketing executive start their search internally, but they often find that their marketers are defined in traditionally narrow ways. The organization has created a self-fulfilling prophecy that prevents it from promoting a marketer from within. At the same time, the organization had created a strategic, customer-led vacuum, pointing to the fact that the company needs to make *The Shift*.

Several influencing factors foreshadow the environment in which a marketer can end up merely operating at the Tactician level versus thriving at the Leader or Visionary Marketer level. In our experience with numerous companies, we've seen that some

Figure I.2 Success Enablers

organizations are more aggressive or strategic in their belief about marketing's role, and others fall back on conventional norms. We have seen four success enablers that dictate the degree to which marketing's success across the four roles will flourish or flounder (Figure I.2):

- *Board and CEO disposition toward Marketing as visionary*. Some Board and CEO dispositions enable *The Shift*. If the Board or CEO starts with an operational or traditional quarter-to-quarter financial mind-set, the odds are against the company's agreeing to a more expansive marketer role at the Visionary level. However, the Board (or CEO) may be willing to lead with a greater customer orientation if their backgrounds are in that area of business. Brian Swette, former Chairman at Burger King and a former eBay and Procter & Gamble marketer, increased the odds that Burger King would welcome an expanded notion of Marketing: "When BK was in the foxhole, we talked about what parts of the organization were required to have the absolute best and brightest staff, in a turnaround situation like ours, and Marketing rose to the top. We didn't compromise, and we recruited the best, gave Marketing the head count, the dollars, and the mandate to change the trajectory." As a result, through an increased focus on Marketing, Burger King has taken off again after several underperforming years.

• *Organizational history and industry dynamics*. Dynamics can enable or inhibit. If the organization, or the industry as a whole, has not appreciated or experienced the value of marketing, then a different kind of challenge is presented to the aspiring senior marketer. Pam Butcher, currently Vice President and General Manager for the Adhesives and Sealants Business at The Dow Chemical Company and Dow's former Corporate Vice President of Marketing and Sales, states, "Dow is traditionally known as an operationally excellent company—science and technology based—but lacking the desired level of customer intimacy. I was named to lead Marketing to really restructure Marketing within the organization. While we are considered to be the best in marketing within the chemical industry, we are not where we want to be relative to leaders in other industries. We are still in our infancy across Dow relative to marketing but beginning to make some significant progress." The dynamics of both the organization and the category or industry it competes in often dictates how steep the climb will be for an aspiring marketer eyeing a more visionary profile.

• *Previous marketing success within the organization*. Success is enabled by the company's previous marketing success or constrained by the lack thereof. Five years ago, Sean Burke, former CMO of GE Healthcare's Diagnostic Imaging Business and current CMO of GE Healthcare, Americas, working without a dedicated marketing budget, muscled his way into creating the business's first true customer segmentation; he knew that without deep customer insight, the business would never hit its growth aspirations. With minimal resources, he led the creation of a robust segmentation of one of the business lines. Showing the business line leaders growth opportunities, as well as savings opportunities due to inefficiencies in how marketing dollars were being allocated across the business, earned him credibility. Burke's success has allowed marketing to continue to be viewed as a true growth catalyst for the company.

- *The expertise, experience, track record, and humility of the individual marketer.* The likelihood of success of the marketer as growth champion also depends on the individual's background and balance of modesty and tenacity.

Consider this story. A few years ago, a major Fortune 500 technology solutions provider brought in its first high-profile marketing executive, partly to address a board concern about the lack of marketing muscle at the company and partly to help drive new leads. This high-profile executive, with a CPG background, came into the company demanding a CMO title instead of the Vice President of Marketing title offered. Within months on the job, he had fired and hired new agencies and tactical partners to redo the logo, the color scheme, and the advertising. In addition, this CMO butted heads with the CEO and the Senior Vice President of Sales, as well as several Board members. Although a few memorable ads were created during his tenure and the color palettes are now standardized throughout the organization, this CMO drove no noticeable top-line value to the organization. In addition, he burned bridges across the C-suite and became famous for everything that the twenty-six-month-tenured CMO usually becomes famous for: no demonstrable value added (and when he was subsequently let go, he walked off with an exit package that left everyone with a bad taste).

Compare that example to the approach Yvonne LaPenotiere took when she moved into her CMO role at Carlson Hotels Worldwide, ultimately becoming the President of the largest operating unit and, culminating her career at the company, running all demand generation as Global Brand Officer. She believes her success stems from the fact that she spent the first year driving overall corporate strategy within the company:

> I came in with credibility tied to my CPG background and having run a P&L before. Early on, I forced uncomfortable conversations about what we wanted to become three to five years out from a brand and strategy perspective. I made sure I showed some early wins (some segments that were not being picked off by the competition), and I built a dialogue with both internal and external operators. Most important, this was never about marketing first; it was about strategy first. Also, I never underestimated how little I knew about the industry at first and how much I needed to partner with others to get to a win-win for the organization.

LaPenotiere clearly knew her strengths and weaknesses and showed respect and humility to the rest of the organization. She recognized her liabilities as an outsider but also leveraged her rich experience and expertise from previous roles. Ironically, her outsider humility quickly paved the path forward, and she became one of the most valued insiders as she helped drive RevPAR (the hotel benchmark for revenue per average room) up by ten points.

One indicator of your potential success in making *The Shift* is where you reside on the continuums in Figure I.2 (p. 10). Another important indicator will be the archetype of your organization.

Can You Shift? Look First at Your Marketing Organization Archetype

The CEO and Board's disposition to Marketing is a powerful enabler or disabler of *The Shift*. As such, to truly understand the potential for a marketer to move from Tactician to Visionary within your company, you need to identify your marketing organization archetype.

Every organization has one. The five described here embody the range of marketing profiles in existence today; your current or prospective organization will most likely align with one of them. Answering the disposition question will help reveal how difficult it will be to shift your profile, as well as the steps you should take to make *The Shift*—and the challenges you might face in doing so.

Archetype I: The Instinctive Marketer's Organization

When a company's founder is an instinctive marketer, it often enjoys phenomenal success. This archetype is exemplified by instinctive marketers such as Howard Schultz of Starbucks, Michael Dell of Dell Computers, Steve Jobs of Apple, Arthur Blank of The Home Depot, Martha Stewart of Martha Stewart Living Omnimedia, Charles Schwab of Charles Schwab Corporation, and Phil Knight of Nike. Each came up with a great, single idea and persevered against the greatest of odds to create world-class, customer-led organizations that disrupted their existing categories through new products, services, or customer experiences.

Interestingly, all of these CEOs tried to turn their companies over to another CEO, often with a financially oriented, operational mind-set. The failure of follow-up CEOs to push their companies to the next level of growth is as legendary as the lives of their founders. In the recent past, we can think of Arthur Blank ceding control to Bob Nardelli at The Home Depot and Steve Jobs's handing off to John Sculley. Because these new CEOs came in with a cost-oriented, operational focus, the organizations lost the passion and inspiration that came from the founders. Eventually many of these legendary CEOs, like Steve Jobs, Howard Schultz, and Michael Dell, came back to run, inspire, innovate, and transform their companies a second time, seeking to add to their market leadership position and ultimately their overall legacy as true visionaries. Only time will tell whether all of these marketing and business legends are able to reclaim their companies' former status . . . and what the impact will be on their own legacies.

Archetype I companies never think about whether Marketing is important to growth. They just know it is. More important, they prove that company leaders can be visionary idea and marketing leaders and great executors simultaneously. To demonstrate that the instinctive phenomenon is not a thing of the past, consider Zappos, a newer company that fits this archetype. CEO Tony Hsieh uses any opportunity to go on record to say that his company is a "service company that happens to sell shoes and clothes" and to inspire the rest of his organization. He spends money on improving the customer experience and ensuring he maintains an inspired culture before he'll spend money on traditional marketing and branding vehicles. Hsieh knows what the brand needs to stand for and continues to build brand equity with a laser focus on the customer and employee base, realizing that "everything else will fall out from there."

Although you may never own the label of Instinctive Marketer, you can borrow many of the concepts that make Instinctive Marketers and their organizations so successful: dogmatic belief in the customer; commitment to an original, disruptive vision; continuous innovation and improvement; cultural leadership; and a support group made up of leaders aligned with your own set of values.

Implications of an Instinctive Marketer's Organization. Perhaps you'd like to jump into an Instinctive Marketer's Organization. Be forewarned, though, that these CEOs will have strong, preconceived notions of their brand and what role Marketing should play, and they often get directly involved in the tactics. Your chance to make your mark will be directly tied to the strength and evolution of your relationship with an Instinctive Marketer CEO. He or she will be your harshest critic and biggest fan, possibly at the same time.

Archetype II: The High-Powered Marketing Organization

These organizations view Marketing and strategic leadership as one and the same. Stereotypically found within classic CPG companies, the High-Powered Marketing Organization generally arrives at the same result from two different starting points.

One starting point may be that the company's CEO is a former marketing star. This is best exemplified by Meg Whitman, formerly of eBay, A. G. Lafley of Procter & Gamble, Bob Harris of LendingTree.com, and Tom Long of Miller. Because many of these stars' original companies were rooted in classic CPG environments, these leaders started out as brand, category, or divisional managers and understood that brand management and business management were one and the same—tied to successfully running a business and delivering the numbers. These senior marketers have always been seen as a natural part of their respective leadership teams, regardless of where they have been employed. Cammie Dunaway, another Visionary Marketer, has an expansive CMO position at Nintendo, as she did at Yahoo! and as she did before that when she ran a major division at Frito-Lay, managing volume and profit growth for a $3.5 billion portfolio. Marketing executives like Dunaway work hand-in-hand with the CEO, executive team, and often the Board, always entering the conversation with a strategic, customer-first mind-set. Based on others previously discussed with her same pedigree, perhaps Dunaway is destined to play a CEO role.

Another, more recent starting point may be that the company's CMO previously ran a P&L. This newer phenomenon may represent a blueprint for the future. Dan Henson ran Sales for GE Commercial Finance before becoming CMO of GE Corporate and, finally, President and CEO of GE Capital Solutions. Similarly, Ranjana Clark, a twenty-year Wachovia star, was plucked from running the Treasury Business to become Wachovia's CMO. In discussing why she moved from line to Marketing, Clark explains:

> Our CEO stretched the marketing responsibilities and the vision of Marketing to include Insight and Innovation, Global Branding, Customer Experience and Loyalty, Marketing Infrastructure, and E-Commerce,

> all built on the discipline of marketing excellence. He wanted to bring in an insider for the CMO role, someone who was a critical thinker, knew the company and culture and the mind-set of our businesses.

Implications of a High-Powered Marketing Organization. The organizational expectations here are high. A strategic mind-set is the conversation starter; being a driver of growth is expected. These are the companies everyone writes about. Marketing as a core, strategic asset is the norm, not the exception. These marketers are generally immune from the CMO "26-month tenure affliction." In fact, they are on most headhunters' lists as candidates for future high-profile Marketing and CEO positions.

Archetype III: The Aspiring Marketing Organization

Rediscovering or discovering for the first time, the power of Marketing, Aspiring Marketing Organizations often receive Board-level approval to ratchet up investments and look for the right leader to help transform the organization. Marketing is often a strategic driver for future success, and finding the right individual is vital.

Burger King is a good example of an Aspiring Marketing Organization. Brian Swette, its former chairman, looked at Marketing as a strategic imperative that the Board and CEO had to get right. He explained, "We brought in Russ Klein as the CMO, and Russ took this charter seriously." Swette likes to tell the story:

> Russ's marketing group clearly understood that we were going through the phase of getting the company going in the right direction after several years of decline. They did anthropological work (into our core customers' likes and dislikes) that went against trends. Based on this work, they created an innovation group that drove a lot of great products and new revenue streams.

Eventually Burger King Corporation and Klein began to make *The Shift* toward becoming a High-Powered Marketing Organization, one in which the marketing function, which they'd always had, was now the growth champion too.

Like Klein and Burger King, many others in the Aspiring Marketing Organization archetype are given more responsibility and organization-wide accountability. This is exemplified by James Farley at Ford, who demanded responsibility for Sales and Marketing in the United States to be in the same pressure cooker as his peers, as well as Rob Malcolm from Diageo, who earned the title of President of Global Marketing, Sales, and Innovation.

In making Marketing a strategic imperative, the Board and CEO of Aspiring Marketing Organizations bring in the best talent, supported with the right level of resources, to lead their organization on a customer-inspired journey. While an Aspiring Marketing Organization today, Walmart is well on its way to becoming a High-Powered Marketing Organization, with Quinn at the marketing helm. As Quinn noted, "If other CMOs knew how much Walmart's Board and executive team were committed to deepening its marketing commitment, I might have had to fight harder for the job."

Implications of the Aspiring Marketing Organization. These organizations provide the greatest number of stretch opportunities for the marketer, as Quinn has realized. Of his company, he admits:

> Walmart was not a strong customer-centric company, but was clearly operationally oriented. After years of studying the customer, we had the courage to boldly drive initiatives. We argued that we knew the customer better than at any other time in Walmart's history. This knowledge gave us the power to define a road map for growth: answering the key questions of which customers to make our focus and what we had to do to serve

> them better. We could see the intersection between what shoppers hired us to do and the capabilities of our company. More important in the short term, we began to kill bad ideas. The company was still approving programs that rated a 5 out of 10 by customers. With our customer knowledge, we could make certain that we only focused on programs rating 9 out of 10.

Like Walmart, other Aspiring Marketing Organizations give their marketers a fairly wide playing field, as well as a longer time frame in which to achieve expected results and the right amount of resources to support success. They can prove to be among the best workplaces in which an aspiring marketer can make his or her mark.

At the same time, of course, these organizations also have the highest expectations and yield the highest risk-return quotient. The Board is watching, the CEO is as accountable for success as is the marketer, and *Advertising Age* is watching closely to see if it should be running a new headline story about CMO attrition anytime soon.

Archetype IV: The Disciplined Marketing Function

As *disciplined* implies, a strong marketer, determined to drive a marketing-led transformation, leads marketing for these organizations. Often the marketer will unleash the power of marketing in a company without a tradition of marketing prowess. Here, the marketer can truly make a mark. When Ruth Fornell ran marketing at Teradata from 2000 to 2003, she helped transform the organization from a sales-led to a customer-led broader-platform organization. Eventually Teradata went from being a successful business unit of NCR (run at the time by Mark Hurd, current CEO of HP) to an incredibly successful spin-off initial public offering tied to its business and brand strength.

Despite the initial lack of marketing acumen, many of these companies realize that Marketing is critical for future growth. As a result, they often look to a marketer to help figure out exactly what the role can become, largely based on the marketer's experience. This senior marketer will drive the marketing agenda, largely from scratch. These marketers will have to frame everything for their respective organizations, from the exact nature of the CMO job description, to the CMO's accountabilities, to the parameters for measuring success.

Not surprisingly, this archetype is often found in sales-led organizations or older-line business-to-business manufacturing and industrial companies that grasp the need for a high-profile, disciplined marketer to lead them on a marketing journey, without exactly knowing where they are going. Pam Butcher was brought into a new corporate marketing role for old-line Dow to shake things up. Even as Butcher has moved out of marketing into a business unit leadership position, many of the recommendations she made in her previous role for advancing marketing are being adopted—clearly a sign of success.

Butcher truly could carve out her own way since this was a new role. As the marketing leader, she could experiment and go where no other Dow marketer had ever gone before. Butcher began to find success in an unlikely place:

> The R&D leaders really get Marketing. Marketing is their license to operate. We now tag-team with R&D to define needs and discuss and prioritize new product opportunities. Our motto is that "Marketing times Technology drives Innovation and Growth." You can't just have Marketing; you also need Technology for the differentiation. We operate as "two in a box"; Marketing and R&D align, and we agree on what needs to be worked on.

Implications of the Disciplined Marketing Function. This archetype, more than any other one, depends on the personality, talent, and tenacity of the leader. The marketer must take on the characteristics of successful growth-oriented marketers, as well as the roles of teacher, leader, "tour guide," and inspirer.

Archetype V: The Old School Marketing Function

In the Old School archetype, the lead marketer is stuck in the traditional marketing role. Often he or she chooses to define marketing's value and success in terms of the old "tagline/logo redo" effort. Ultimately this archetype will most likely continue to reinforce the company's narrow definition of Marketing and thus will be seen as "a success" because the organization gets exactly what it asks for: a strong Marketing Tactician.

Implications of the Old School Marketing Function. If tactical marketing communication execution is seen as a win-win, this may work for this company and the marketer. The Visionary Marketer can never win in this company, regardless of how hard he or she pushes, because the organization has been normed into an old-school way of thinking about Marketing. Only a complete organizational overhaul can change this entrenched point of view.

Table I.1 summarizes the archetypes.

Archetypes and Success Enablers Combine to Show the Best

By integrating your judgments about your company's enablers and archetype, you can get a glimpse of your potential: the level of marketing success you are likely to reach, as well as the type of marketing leadership required to reach each level of success (Table I.2). You can also begin to surface hypotheses to address questions that may arise where different archetypes prevail—for example:

> "Can the marketer in Archetype IV shift his organization's marketing perspective based on lessons learned from the other marketing archetypes?"

Table I.1 Organizational Archetypes

Archetype	Characteristics	Implications for Head of Marketing
Archetype I: Instinctive Marketer's Organization	Organization is driven by the original marketer Marketing is defined by the original vision of the Visionary CEO Dogmatic belief in the customer	Difficult to break free of expectations set by Visionary CEO Must have a positive relationship with Visionary CEO
Archetype II: High-Powered Marketing Organization	Marketing and strategic leadership are equally valued CEO is a former or established marketer, or CMO formally ran a P&L	Expected to have strategic /P&L conversations Drive growth within the organization
Archetype III: Aspiring Marketing Organization	Organization discovered or rediscovered the power of marketing recently The Board and CEO have prioritized Marketing as a strategic imperative with Board approval and resources	Given a wide playing field yet narrow time frame to achieve results Under strict watch to meet expectations
Archetype IV: Disciplined Marketing Function	Marketing function is driven by a strong, individual marketer who is determined to lead change Marketing is new to the organization	Must teach and lead the organization
Archetype V: Old School Marketing Function	Narrow definition of Marketing, defined by traditional marketing communication responsibilities	Responsible for traditional marketing communications tactics Not likely to elevate role beyond these responsibilities

"What can marketers in Archetype III do to succeed and help their companies turn into Archetype I or II companies?"

"Can a marketer in Archetype I really succeed given the omnipresence of the Instinctive Marketing Leader within the organization?"

The answer to these questions? "Maybe."

Even with this transparency into what your success profile might be, something is missing from this discussion—something that will guarantee that the marketing profile will forever shift and something that will help to turbocharge the elevation of Marketer as Tactician to marketer as Visionary, possibly cutting through all the archetypes.

There are five shifts that will change the marketing dialogue forever and entrench the term *Visionary Marketer* into the marketing lexicon for good. These shifts, as previously surfaced, include:

- *Shift One: From creating marketing strategies to driving business impact*. Chapter One discusses the importance of elevating the marketing dialogue to a strategic dialogue, inspired by the organization's longer-term goal and objectives. It also suggests several strategies that Visionary Marketers can employ immediately to alter the dialogue permanently.
- *Shift Two: From controlling the message to galvanizing your network*. Chapter Two discusses the importance of recognizing that controlling the customer experience and perceptions of your brand is no longer the end game for marketers. Visionary Marketers recognize that customers reside within a complex web of influencers. The objective now is to control what you can and influence all else.
- *Shift Three: From incremental improvements to pervasive innovation*. Chapter Three explores how Visionary

Table I.2 Leadership Profiles

		Archetype I: Instinctive Marketer's Organization	Archetype II: High-Powered Marketing Organization	Archetype III: Aspiring Marketing Organization	Archetype IV: Disciplined Marketing Function	Archetype V: Old School Marketing Function
Success Enablers	CEO/Board disposition	CEO/Board is in full support; original marketer is often the founder or CEO who has defined the brand and role of marketing for the company	CEO/Board is in full support, as Marketing and strategic leadership are valued the same	CEO/Board has recently discovered marketing and has prioritized marketing as a strategic initiative	CEO/Board sees the potential for Marketing to contribute to growth but relies on the marketer to define that role	CEO/Board has a historical mind-set and limits the definition of marketing to traditional marketing communication role
	Organizational history/industry dynamics	Organization embraces Marketing and its role in strategic discussions	Organization embraces Marketing and its role in strategic discussions	Organization is aware of the value of Marketing and is actively seeking the best marketer for the role	Organization is aware of the value of Marketing but does not know how to define the role	The organization or the industry (or both) has yet to see the value that Marketing can add

Success Enablers	Previous Marketing success	Organization has seen the value of Marketing in its bottom-line results	Organization has seen the value of Marketing in its bottom-line results	Organization has seen marketing-led successes in other companies and is ready to invest its resources	Organization has yet to see robust results from marketing efforts but is open to a broader role	Organization has yet to see bottom-line results from marketing efforts outside marketing communication results
	Individual marketer traits	Strategic Visionary Influencer Risk taker	Strategic Visionary Influencer Risk taker	Collaborator Pragmatic Resourceful	Collaborator Resourceful Results oriented	Results oriented Task oriented Short-term mind-set
	Most probable leadership profile	Visionary: leads strategic growth discussions; however, may still need final approval by founder/CEO	Visionary: leads strategic growth discussions, which is in line with CEO/board expectations	Leader: serves up strategic issues and opportunities since Marketing is prioritized as a strategic initiative	Facilitator: develops a common language around brand and facilitates discussions around best practices	Tactician: focuses on traditional marketing communication responsibilities, which is in line with the CEO/ board expectations

Marketers can help lead their organization's desire to continuously innovate across all aspects of the business, leveraging all internal and external assets on an ongoing basis and keeping the business fresh and relevant in the minds of all customers and influencers.

- *Shift Four: From managing marketing investments to inspiring marketing excellence*. Chapter Four looks at how Visionary Marketers have to be focused on maximizing their investments across all of Philip Kotler's 4 P's of Marketing, appropriately dialing up and down all investments made to win over customers' hearts and minds.
- *Shift Five: From an operational focus to a relentless customer focus*. Chapter Five discusses how Visionary Marketers can inspire their organizations to lead, manage, and influence with the customer at the center of their organization's universe—in effect, disregarding traditional organizational silos and history.

Each of the five shifts is powerful and game changing for marketers and their organizations. Taken together, these five shifts provide an organization with a source of competitive advantage that may become insurmountable for the competition.

I

THE FIRST SHIFT

From Creating Marketing Strategies to Driving Business Impact

Ranjana Clark, former CMO at Wachovia and now Head, Wholesale Customer Experience Group at Wells Fargo, shared her story about her realization that a shift was going to occur at the bank. She knew that the company needed Marketing to play more of a strategic role. But what did that mean?

> My first charge was not to freshen up the brand or build a new campaign. I realized then and there that my charter would be different from that of my predecessors and that I was going to be counted on to be one of the architects of business strategy for Wachovia.

Ultimately Clark made *The Shift* to business impact, pulling out all of the stops to become a strategic architect for Wachovia. How did she make this shift—and how can you?

She began in a way that you as an aspiring Visionary Marketer can learn from. By working your way through a definable set of

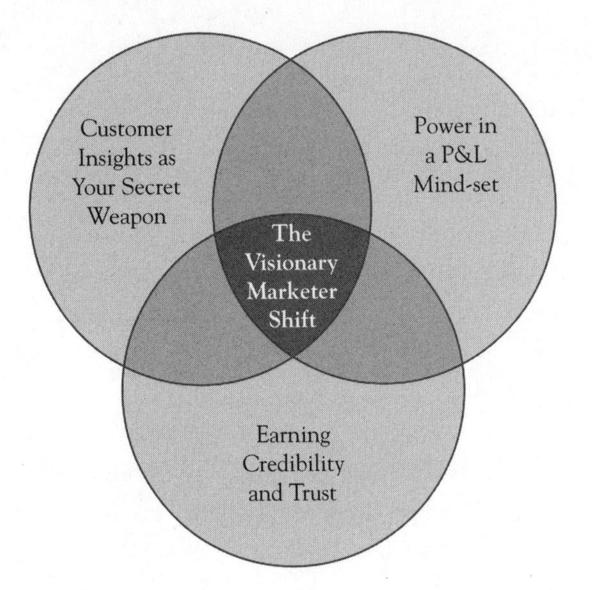

Figure 1.1 The First Shift

actions, with an awareness of your organization's receptivity to change, you can develop the mind-set, track record, and capabilities necessary to prove your abilities to tackle business strategy—not just marketing strategies—and drive business impact. Three critical elements are needed to start to make this shift from creating marketing strategies to driving business impact: leveraging customer insights as your secret weapon, always operating with a profit-and-loss mind-set, and earning organization-wide credibility and trust (Figure 1.1).

Insights: Your Secret Weapon

In order to make this power shift toward driving the growth agenda, most of the senior marketers interviewed for this book said they believed they benefited from knowledge they had that no one else in their organization understood. "Our secret weapon," Barry Judge, CMO of Best Buy, called it. "Customer insights are used as a catalyst for a marketing revolution." Fully owning this secret weapon means both knowing your customer better than any other executive *and* consistently translating this knowledge into actionable consumer insights and in-market execution. You can wield this tool in every discussion and debate on strategy as well as tactics, and in the process, you will gain respect as well as an enhanced organizational profile.

At Staples, CMO Shira Goodman uses customer insights to drive decision making across every functional area, including nontraditional areas such as operations and merchandising. The powerful "hassle-free shopping" insight was translated into an enormously successful "easy" strategy that Goodman then used to collaborate with her peers and guide all aspects of the business. Customer knowledge and insights have changed how Staples is run, from advertising and communications messages to store layout and product assortment.

Stephen Quinn, CMO of Walmart, began from a similar base:

> We knew early on that if we didn't start with the customer and enter into every strategic and tactical discussion grounded in customer insights, then we would not move the needle. This was tough, as Walmart had not been all that customer-centric, having made Operations the backbone of the company. Customer data and insights gave us courage and a convincing hand in determining what was fact and what was fiction. And it drove ideas for growth. For example, when we discovered that pharmacy customers routinely broke pills in half because they couldn't afford their full prescription, we developed the very successful $4 prescription program. With knowledge, we had the power to define growth in a much more relevant way. The use of insights was more powerful than I had ever hoped it could have been at Walmart.

The importance of customer insight helped Barry Judge begin to make his mark on Best Buy. As he remembers, "They were having difficulty operationalizing the customer-centric strategy . . . generating growth through a customer lens." Judge stepped in because he had a "different point of view on growth" from anyone else in the company at that time. Once he harnessed the customer insights, he helped Best Buy develop "a unique perspective, looking across all of our segments and all of our product categories and all of our geographies. Instead of looking for product categories to add in or expand to, we are now always looking at the needs our consumers are trying to fulfill and what the benefit is that they can't seem to get to."

Bob Harris, now President of the LendingTree Exchange, concurs and has been able to reflect back to his own tenure as a marketing officer at LendingTree, The Coca-Cola Company, and elsewhere. Harris's perspective is that the marketing leader needs to see new opportunities for growth based on customer insights . . . and needs to see that sooner than the CEO does. They must have a strong voice and sense of responsibility for providing deep knowledge and insight into making all major strategic decisions, from new products to acquisitions to new segments to pursue.

Based on their customer knowledge, marketers have an opportunity now to enhance their power. They can use this asset to reposition Marketing to drive enterprisewide growth and conduct customer-led strategic discussions and debates.

Of course, it isn't easy to instill customer insight as an asset into an organization that is not predisposed to thinking about Marketing as the repository of customer insight. In some companies, customer insight teams are positioned as lower-level, analytically oriented teams reporting up to the marketing communication group, tied only to improving its tactical strategies. You will need to reposition these teams based on a new asset-oriented view of these insights.

As these examples suggest, Marketing at a minimum should become the repository, integrator, and ultimately disseminator of all proprietary and syndicated data, research, and tracking studies across the organization. The best CMOs turn this minimum expectation into an insight machine, cutting through all of the data and reports that most others never read. In fact, no other function but Marketing comes closer to the customer, with a deep, intertwined perspective across all segments, needs states, geographies, and demographics. Visionary Marketers recognize they must not only provide the economic rationale for building a world-class insight team but also outline the economic opportunities tied to each of the insights they are bringing to the organization.

Just as these executives recognize that data without insights are meaningless, they also recognize that insights without economic perspective will not be valued. This reality leads to the need for a P&L mind-set.

Power in a P&L Mind-Set

Must you own a P&L to establish credibility and drive true peer-to-peer relationships, or can you develop a P&L mind-set without ever actually owning an income statement? I argue that you do not need to own a P&L in order to succeed. What really matters is that day in and day out, you consistently have a perspective and action orientation based on an understanding of how the company makes money, how investment decisions in one area impact others, and always bring a top- and bottom-line perspective to the decisions at hand. That is what we mean by a "P&L mind-set."

Stephen Quinn at Walmart is emphatic that growth-oriented marketing leaders need a P&L mind-set, but they do not necessarily need to own one to have this mind-set. Quinn effectively articulates this difference between having a P&L mind-set versus actual P&L ownership:

> In many packaged goods companies, the P&L is jointly shared, but there is a P&L for each brand, and the brand manager runs it. So I grew up with the belief that running a P&L is part of being a marketer. However, at the

> time I was considering taking a position at Walmart, I read an article by brand marketing guru David Aaker [Vice Chairman of Prophet] about the average twenty-six-month tenure of CMOs. He predicted that P&L owners would continue to struggle. However, those who were freed up from running the P&L and allowed to truly focus on the customer could add so much more value to their company. Time spent on forecasts, financial planning, reporting systems, and the like could be allocated to becoming leaders of the customer inside their organization. From my perspective, the customer will always be more important than controlling the P&L, but without mastering the dynamics of the P&L, you will not have the credibility to initiate the types of conversations that you really need to grow the business.

Other CMOs embrace owning P&Ls as an important part of their job description. Nabil Shabshab of JohnsonDiversey, Becky Saeger of Charles Schwab, and Ann Lewnes of Adobe believe that owning a P&L is a natural extension of Marketing's go-to-market strategy, one that helps build growth credibility. Lewnes is passionate about this:

> I own traditional marketing, and I also have P&L responsibility for the education segment, which is the largest vertical at Adobe, as well as the P&L for e-commerce. That puts me on the hook in a big way, and I am okay with that, as I think having P&L responsibility makes you more credible. More important, owning a P&L forces you to be more conversant in your own business, diffusing any complaints that Marketing just doesn't get it or doesn't have business acumen. Bottom line, you need to be able to understand the product and the customer in an

> intimate way to be a credible resource for the business. Owning a P&L helps you get there.

Whether or not you've owned a P&L, it's most important to understand your organization's P&L, buy into the importance of the accountability level expected of those running the P&Ls, have the ability to drive profitable programs, and know how to help prioritize and drive success in the target customer segments that ultimately help to drive margin.

If you are still a Tactician or Facilitator Marketer, it's time you started to understand the need to adopt a different profile and mind-set in order to become a Visionary Marketer. By having a P&L mind-set, you will make it harder—nearly impossible—for your peers to dismiss you. They will see you permanently through a different lens that says "enterprisewide leader."

As Dennis Cary, Chief Marketing and Customer Officer at United Airlines, put it, "A P&L orientation will always enhance the credibility and support you receive from your executive peers." Cary explained how he shifted his own mind-set:

> When I took this job, I didn't have as much accountability for revenue as my sales or revenue management peers. Having a commercial lens, using data and insights to build loyalty and attract new customers, was my mind-set. However, having customer needs tethered to a clear pathway for how these insights affect revenue, profitability, and ultimately shareholder value, it changes the conversation between Marketing and the rest of the organization, including the CFO, CEO, and Board of Directors, in a very healthy way. We are now more involved in every aspect of demand generation and top-line growth. In fact, my boss is the Chief Operating Officer, and Marketing is one of his primary enablers.

As a corollary to the P&L discussion, whichever side of ownership you and your company land on, the importance of understanding the language of, and collaborating with, the CFO cannot be underestimated. Beth Comstock of GE believes strongly that marketers must connect strategy and vision to financials and the P&L: "I am a fan of marketers partnering with the CFO. The CFO wants to grow and will be your best friend if they think you are helping them."

This Visionary Marketer is clearly on to something. According to an article by B. Johnson in *Advertising Age*, "Survey Finds CFOs Skeptical of Their Own Firms' ROI Claims," six in ten financial executives believe their companies' marketing departments have an inadequate understanding of financial controls, and seven in ten said their companies don't use marketing inputs and forecasts in financial guidance to Wall Street or in public disclosures.

Yvonne LaPenotiere, of Carlson Hotels, combats this prejudice by starting a different type of dialogue—a strategic one:

> Throughout our strategy development, my marketing team and I always tied our recommendations to a pretty rigorous business case and the commensurate financial results. Metrics such as revenue per average room index [RevPAR] was the language of our CFO and CEO, and any other measure or metric-like language would never have passed the C-suite test. We engaged them in their language, not traditional marketing-speak.

At the end of the day, marketers who have made *The Shift* will consistently make sure Marketing is contributing to the P&L. They will recommend and push marketing programs and efforts that help the business, and they will want their performance metrics and bonus payouts tied to business performance measurements, just like any other senior executive. Steve Meyer of Dell Services says Dell Marketing is "incented on business, return-on-investment-type metrics." LaPenotiere said that when she was with Carlson, "70% of her bonus was based on the financial results of Carlson Hotels Worldwide"—the same as the CEO.

With these first two pieces in place—strategic insights and a P&L mind-set—you will have begun to redefine the role of Marketing within the organization and transform Marketing from not just enabling growth through world-class marketing but driving it. You will become one of the true reasons to believe within the organization and you will have successfully started on the road to earning organizational credibility and trust.

Cementing the First Shift: Earning Organizational Credibility and Trust

Now that you're ready to become a marketing leader, there is no better advice than that of Adam Stotsky, President of NBC Entertainment Marketing and former Senior Vice President of Marketing for the Sci-Fi Channel. Stotsky has become a marketing leader by virtue of his success in driving his company's growth agenda. He speaks from experience:

> The only way marketers are going to get that seat at the [CEO] table is by building and earning credibility and trust. They need to understand the totality of the business, have a deeply informed opinion, and look at different ways of adding value beyond the sphere of marketing. Far too many CMOs come to the role with only knowledge about communications and advertising. Credibility and trust are built through in-depth [knowledge] throughout the value chain—from the customer to product development to the supply chain and everything in between.

In some ways, cultivating this new mind-set runs against the grain of most marketers. You will have to succeed at basic marketing communication tactics *and* show muscle in resolving complex business issues. You must unemotionally analyze your budget to make trade-offs within the context of the goals of the overall organization. At the same time, you'll have to be comfortable in driving or codriving all of the elements of the traditional purchase funnel, from awareness through loyalty, incorporating all of Phil Kotler's 4 P's.

For the first time within many organizations, marketing's playbook will include objectively making trade-offs on whether the company should initiate a print campaign, hire more sales representatives, invest in greater innovation efforts, or expand into a new geography.

Leveraging customer insights and having a P&L mind-set will start the transformation. Visionary Marketers have used these weapons wisely to earn organization-wide credibility and trust, cementing their position with the broader leadership team.

Becky Saeger agrees that this is the best way to get where you want to go: "I had to run a strong team, grow the business, and show results. If you are on the team solely as a marketer, then you will never be viewed as a critical strategic player unless you have that credibility and trust." Bob Harris put it this way: "I have always tried to be viewed as someone who can take strategy and execute against it. The credibility comes from execution so that you are not perceived as coming up with only strategy or only execution. You can do both. You can integrate insights from the marketplace into in-market strategies and tactics, which gave me more credibility and, in turn, helped me build trust throughout the organization."

Obviously the gap between where you are today and building credibility and trust tomorrow can be quite wide depending on your company's archetype and your position on the Visionary Marketer spectrum—like having the right mind-set, skill set, strategic awareness, and desire to address the challenge head on. Visionary

Marketers agree that in the quest to garner credibility and trust, there are four success factors to help change the dialogue and shift marketing's overall profile:

1. *Understand the business inside and out*. "Become" an operator: spend considerable time in the field with both employees and customers, and understand the inner workings of every functional area and how they make money. The deeper your understanding is of the profit pools from an internal and external perspective, the more strategic you will appear.
2. *Conduct any business dialogue from a strategic, not a tactical or even marketing, perspective*. Be ready to demonstrate precisely how your ideas will enhance and drive specific growth imperatives.
3. *Form the right alliances*. Recognize that strong Sales, Finance, Human Resources, Information Technology, and business unit relations can help to raise your credibility.
4. *Search for small wins; put skin in the game*. Both Best Buy and Carlson have diverted traditional marketing funds into enhancing the customer and employee experiences when those were determined to have the greatest impact on business results.

The Visionary Marketers we spoke with were quick to stress the importance of these, with none more important than the obvious, yet not so easy, "Understand the business inside and out."

Steve Meyer of Dell was clear that there are definite boundaries on a marketers' impact if one stays in the insular realm of outbound communications. Tom O'Toole's experience at Hyatt reinforced this perspective. As the former CMO and CIO of Hyatt said, "My personal credibility grew enormously when I had a deep understanding of the business, how we made money, who our customers and operators were. This dramatically changed the dialogue."

Barry Judge makes an important distinction between the traditional marketing mind-set and that of the Visionary Marketer:

> Once you understand the business and how you make money, you will start to become immune from grandstanding for what Marketing just does. You will start labeling your budget as a growth budget—and not an advertising or marketing communication budget. You will assert that you will deploy those dollars to drive the business—by pilot testing, doing more training, putting up new stores, killing initiatives. I put our money where we have the best chance of improving the overall business.

What Meyer, O'Toole, and Judge are speaking about is earning the credibility and confidence a marketer must have to engage in a more growth-oriented dialogue about the business. For each, the ability to start to engage at this level started with an understanding of the organization from the bottom up, inside and out. Each spent time in the field "working the registers," understanding the economics, and having well-rounded discussions about what is best for the company and how to consistently balance the need for short- and long-term success.

A case study on the following page brings all of these elements together: insights, P&L mind-set, credibility, and trust.

How to Set the Growth Agenda

"Any strong head of marketing wants to own the growth agenda," says Steve Meyer, "exploring where we have the best market opportunities, where we have permission to play, and how we can win." If you buy the premise of *The Shift*, then you most likely buy Meyer's words. You know that in every company, Marketing must earn the right to be at the strategy table and help set, or own, the growth agenda. This rite of passage extends from proving you can

A Case Study: Shift from Creating Marketing Strategies to Driving Business Impact

Historically Wachovia viewed customer knowledge as a marketing communications asset—something without significant strategic value. But during her tenure as CMO, Ranjana Clark changed this by elevating the perceived value of Marketing. She recalls, "Our ultimate goal was to create an insight-driven culture. The Marketing Division needed to become the funnel for taking all the external information and knowledge, along with our own experiences and observations, [and] turn all of that into customer insights that could help drive strategic decisions."

Clark accomplished this goal by creating three different marketing teams, or "pods":

> One pod was business-facing, delivering marketing to our different lines of businesses.
>
> The second pod was called Marketing Centers of Excellence. Within this second pod, there were three areas of focus:
>
> - Insight and innovation (customer analytics, targeting). We took all of the insights and drove them into business strategies and executional programs. It also included innovation as a small piece. We didn't feel [that] innovation could be driven centrally, but we certainly knew we could be an innovation catalyst through our insights.
> - Global branding—traditional elements such as advertising, media, sponsorships, brand management. This is still important to our business but could not define Marketing on its own.
> - Customer experience and loyalty. Since our brand is the experience you are delivering at different customer touch points, we wanted to make sure that we were both tracking the touch points and coming up with different experiences to increase loyalty.

The third pod was marketing infrastructure. Marketing excellence is what we do with all of the information we gather on our clients, and the infrastructure is how we actually get the data. So much of this is increasingly becoming online, so e-commerce became part of our sphere of responsibility.

The reality is that we restructured the marketing group and created this three-pod structure to mirror our strategy. In my first sixty days in this position, we developed the marketing and business vision and strategy. We wanted to be the industry leader in innovation, brand differentiation, and loyalty. When we set that vision, we knew the structure needed to follow.

---

execute the basics flawlessly; to earning respect and trust from your peers for the depth of customer insights you bring to the table; to gaining credibility with large and small marketing wins; to being seen as a visionary, risk taker but not as an isolationist.

To earn that seat at the C-table, you will need to spend years within the business or in similar roles in other businesses, or, as Pam Butcher from Dow says, spend a significant amount of time with your customers: "A single year engaging with customers equals a lifetime of other types of learning."

Once you're at the table, you are likely to wonder:

"What role should I play?"

"How can I add the right amount of value to the organization without stepping on toes?"

"What role do the Board and CEO consider the most helpful in driving the organization forward?"

The best marketers know that together, the Visionary Marketer, the CEO, and the Board will ultimately determine what role they see Marketing playing in setting the growth agenda.

Should Marketing own the growth agenda? A range of opinions on this question came from the interviews. Russ Klein of Burger King Corporation may offer a rare point of clarity in the debate. His role, in effect, is to be Chief Growth Officer. He also "believes the premise of [this] book is being lived at Burger King Corporation."

Klein sees himself as a true partner with the CEO, John Chidsey. His expansive purview gives his team and him the stature and recognition to support broad-based growth. Not coincidentally, like all other officers in the company, Klein receives a bonus based on EBITDA (earnings before interest, taxes, depreciation, and amortization) goals and, thus, is motivated to constantly think about cash flow drivers and company performance, both within and outside a traditional marketing lens.

Bob Harris has moved in this direction at LendingTree:

> The buck stops with the CEO. However, the marketing leader should be part of the CEO's inner circle, with a strong voice and sense of responsibility for the knowledge and input required to make key strategic decisions based on customer insights. In the end, marketers should see the big growth opportunities sooner than the rest of the organization, including the CEO, with an eye on what the company should do to be relevant in the future. The CEO needs someone like this because the CEO has too many other tasks on which to focus, both near-in and further-out.

Do Harris and Klein reflect a trend? It depends on your point of view. Meyer observed that "there appears to be a strong movement within many CEO and Board ranks, tied to wanting stronger marketing insight in strategy. . . . While Marketing might not lead the growth agenda alone, it definitely should be a co-conspirator."

Becky Saeger truly believes in the need for marketers to make a shift by changing their profile and becoming much more engaged in strategic discussions. However, she is also quick to add that she thinks complete ownership of the growth agenda takes it too far:

> At Schwab, you can't rely on one person. Sometimes I read this stuff about making the CMO the Chief Growth Officer, and my strong belief is that you need to have a management team in place that can own growth together. It is the same debate that CMOs will often wrongly get entangled in by saying they own the brand. They can't own the brand alone and manage it any more than a marketer should own the growth agenda alone.

To Saeger's point, it would be foolhardy to assume Marketing should be the primary or singular engineer of growth, exclusive to other core drivers of the business, such as the business unit and functional heads. Companies live and die tied to the quality of their offerings, the services surrounding those offerings, the market conditions, and the successful execution of their strategy. That's the reason that many of the marketers interviewed for this book had a visceral aversion to the idea of becoming the sole owner of the growth agenda or the singular co-conspirator alongside the CEO.

Regardless of which of these perspectives you adopt, the ownership for growth has to be shared across the organization, and the Visionary Marketer needs to be a core facilitator of this co-owned growth perspective in the organization. As one CMO aptly put it, "I would be fearful of marketers owning the growth agenda on their own, as it would totally undermine the idea that you live and die with the success of your executive team. Similar to sports, where it is rare for the Most Valuable Player to come from a last-place team, it is rare for a strong marketer in a successful company to be seen as the singular growth partner for the CEO."

If you want to be part of the growth agenda, your next job will be to figure out how best to enter the strategic dialogue.

Aligning Business and Marketing Strategies

You cannot join the growth agenda discussion unless you have something to contribute. The Visionary Marketers interviewed for this book discussed a variety of avenues and conversation starters by which Marketing can credibly open the door and make the most of the opportunity. Remember, you are trying to go where few marketers have gone in the past.

To this point, research has proven that Marketing does not ordinarily speak this growth language, nor does it come naturally to most marketers. A recent study conducted by the Association of National Advertisers/Booz Allen found a significant misalignment between the priorities of chief executives and those of their Chief Marketing Officers. The study showed that while CEOs continue to focus on top- and bottom-line growth and operational efficiencies, CMOs listed four out of their top five priorities as grounded in tactical goals, such as setting global branding guidelines and standards. The study basically concluded that many marketers continued to drift further from influence and, ultimately, the CEO.

This gap was revealed also in Prophet's recent *State of Marketing Study* in which marketers acknowledged that they continue to play a minimal role in the areas of the business that most closely touch the customer—the ones considered integral to continued business growth. As a result, and in order to become part of the growth discussion, there needs to be a realignment, or a first-time alignment, of business strategy and marketing strategy.

If you accept the observation that business strategies and plans and marketing strategies and plans do not often align then you will likely also agree that for marketing to help ultimately drive business impact, it needs to work backward, beginning by aligning growth and marketing objectives. In other words, start with the longer-term goal in mind first and then work back to what that means from a marketing strategy and planning perspective. This is new territory for most marketers, who rarely set their marketing objectives by working backward from macro business objectives like building a presence in China or raising customer retention rates by 20%.

More often than not, marketing strategies and budgets are built and allocated based on a percentage of sales and an increase of *x*% over last year's budget. As such, most marketers work on a go-forward basis, starting the dialogue around this question: "What do we, as marketers, want to get done next fiscal year, based on what we accomplished last year?" They rarely connect their ideas with the goals housed in the longer-term growth strategy.

Once the disconnect is discovered, usually after the fiscal year has started, marketing executives often scramble to shift spending and strategy to align more closely with the business strategy and objectives, attempting to get air cover. So they respond like this: "Oh, you want to build a presence in China this year? Then let me shift some of my brand and marketing dollars to China." The usual result is that although dollars and priorities may shift, Marketing's reputation of being disconnected from the business gets solidified. By contrast, working backward sends a clear change signal to peers, the CEO, and the Board that your marketing strategy and commensurate plans, activities, and tactics will be directly tied to the growth agenda and priorities.

Capturing the CEO's Imagination

By connecting Marketing to corporate strategy, marketers can capture the imagination of the C-suite. Many CEOs have a narrow idea about what Marketing should do, and therefore would not consider marketers to be part of the strategic dialogue. As we discuss throughout this book, this presents a great opportunity for marketers to step up.

Ranjana Clark did just that as Wachovia CMO, engaging the CEO and C-suite in a much broader strategic dialogue—most likely because that is where she came from prior to taking the CMO position:

> My team brought in fresh ideas of what Marketing could become by leading a strategic dialogue to suggest aligning

> corporate-marketing and corporate-strategic objectives, as well as becoming a leader in the more pervasive and broader dialogue at the corporate strategy level. We proved that Marketing could step up and use consumer insights, competitive intelligence, and its broader understanding of the business to drive the dialogue on what the strategic priorities should be.

As you think about engaging your CEO and C-suite in a broader strategic dialogue, you should consider your areas of expertise, the unique knowledge you bring to the table, and, most important, the type of dialogue in which the CEO engages at the Board level, which generally revolves around five macro objectives:

- Increasing shareholder value
- Driving smart and efficient growth
- Improving operational efficiency
- Inspiring the talent base
- Reinventing the business

The more you are able to connect to the Board-level agenda, the more you will help to shift traditional perceptions around what Marketing can, and should, do. To start, the CMOs we interviewed suggest twelve strategic growth topics that could "easily" be marketing led, and all ladder back up to a broader, more macro-level Board dialogue.

Visionary Marketers' Twelve Strategic Growth Topics

The following twelve strategic growth topics, set out in Table 1.1, will allow you to enter into deeper, strategic discussions with your C-level peers and help your organization align on what the priorities should be that Marketing or another function or team should take on. If you start any dialogue around growth with one of these twelve, your strategic profile will change because each is directly

Table 1.1 Categorizing the Twelve Strategic Growth Topics

Increase Shareholder Value	Drive Smart and Efficient Growth	Improve Operational Efficiency	Inspire the Talent Base	Reinvent the Business
1. Building a superior reputation 2. Bridging the today-tomorrow growth gap: balancing growth in the core and planting seeds for the future	3. Optimizing Marketing across Kotler's 4 P's 4. Focusing the organization by building deeper relationships with the highest-margin and highest-potential target customer segments 5. Exploiting intelligent, real-time, customer-data technologies	6. Rationalizing the brand portfolio to focus on building fewer, stronger brands 7. Simplifying and coordinating the selling process	8. Inspiring the organization with a world-class marketing strategy and engagement plan	9. Managing the innovation pipeline as a true portfolio 10. Cultivating a broad internal and external network 11. Inspiring the marketplace with a galvanizing platform and big idea 12. Putting the customer at the center of the universe

tied to one of the five Board-level imperatives mentioned above. Therefore, each is valued at the top and will help to showcase marketing's wider strategic aperture. Quite literally, you can open the conversation, within the C-suite, by stating, "We could drive greater business impact by . . ." and then finishing the sentence with one of the following Twelve Strategic Growth Topics:

1. Building a Superior Reputation

Strengthening the preference for and opinion of the company while insulating it from the impact of negative events tied to all of its stakeholders is of utmost importance for all companies. Very few companies have a single person directly accountable for managing and leading this. It therefore clearly presents an opportunity, and a challenge, for Marketing.

Suzanne McCarron, General Manager, Public Affairs, has to think about Marketing and corporate reputation at Exxon Mobil every day. Managing Exxon Mobil's CSR (corporate social responsibility) is one of the toughest jobs around, but her job helps to remind stakeholders about the good the company is doing. McCarron states, "In many ways, a company's CSR efforts are directly related to corporate reputation or brand reputation—without a doubt, the single most important element of how your company is viewed by customers, employees, potential employees, business partners, and more." She constantly makes sure the world knows about the positive developments in reducing emissions that Exxon Mobil is exploring, while working with *American Idol* to fight malaria in Africa (*Idol Gives Back*) and supporting the Educating Women and Girls Initiative to investments in education and development in Third World countries. Importantly, she is as concerned with Exxon Mobil's corporate reputation as she is with its brand positioning and business line positioning. And, like a strong brand positioning, she believes that a corporation's long-term, lasting reputation is observable, measurable, and directly related to business performance.

2. Bridging the Today-Tomorrow Growth Gap: Balancing Growth in the Core with Planting Seeds for the Future

I noted in my previous book, *Brand Asset Management*, that Marketing has an opportunity to help fill in the growth gap—the difference between revenues today, aspirational revenues tomorrow, and expected declines within the base business—by precisely detailing the strategies that will help fill in the gaps. Whether you build your plan around new segments, new geographies, new offerings, mergers and acquisitions, or increasing the sales force, Marketing has an opportunity to lead the organization through this exercise. If done well, the exercise can act as a prelude to a longer-term strategic discussion or be a by-product of a well-articulated five-year strategy.

The topic of the growth gap will be discussed in more detail in the Third Shift.

3. Optimizing Marketing Across Kotler's 4 P's

At the end of the day sophisticated marketers know that their number one job is simultaneous retention of current customers, acquisition of new customers, and building share of wallet. There must be a constant search for new ways to deliver the necessary financial results. Marketing's responsibility is to have an impact on all sales drivers by holistically understanding what drives awareness, consideration, preference, purchase, and loyalty across segments to ultimately leverage the right set of marketing and selling tools across the 4 P's and maximize return on investment. Chris Gibson, CMO of UnitedHealthcare, is a growth-oriented marketer. She is equally motivated to add fifty sales reps in the western region, fund a sponsorship important to the agent base, look at new product offerings, or support aggressive pricing strategies. Gibson's goal is world-class customer acquisition and retention, not world-class marketing creative and communications.

This topic of optimizing marketing across the 4 P's will be discussed in depth in the Fourth Shift.

4. Focusing the Organization by Building Deeper Relationships with Your Highest-Margin and Highest-Potential Target Customer Segments

The analysis of this growth topic should include needs, wants, attitudes, behaviors, spending patterns, decision-making criteria, brand perceptions, and size of the prize opportunity for all customers, housed within specific customer segments. Such sophisticated segmentation is one of the most underused and underappreciated assets in organizations; however, dividing the customer world into simple yet powerful segments has proven to be an invaluable exercise for countless companies.

Such segmentation, done well, provides organizations with a deep and accurate customer understanding and targeting tool. Companies such as Best Buy and Staples are famous for clearly articulating what it will take to win with each customer segment and what one more share of wallet point means for each of their high-profile segments. The real objective behind this growth imperative is tied to the marketing priorities of focusing on attracting and retaining profitable customers and achieving a greater share of wallet by deeply understanding these customers, what they want and need, and what it will take to wrestle them away from the competition.

Too many organizations conduct a segmentation exercise and then treat it as just that, an exercise, ultimately creating an incredibly expensive PowerPoint deck. If you are going down the segmentation path, leading to, in effect, building your organization around the segments that drive margin, be ready to execute against the recommendations or fear being accused of wasting a lot of your company's valuable time and resources.

5. Exploiting Intelligent, Real-Time Customer-Data Technologies

These technologies can help monitor customer activity, provide real-time information about different marketing tools and efforts, allow you to make real-time decisions and take real-time actions, all potentially leading to increased sales and greater loyalty. You want to become the company that knows more about the customer than your competitor does. This is how Harrah's has done it, with CEO Gary Loveman, a former Harvard Business School professor, leading the charge. As Loveman outlined in Larry Kahaner's book *Competitive Intelligence*, Harrah's can track, monitor, assess, and influence each of its customer segments as it moves through casinos, knowing the specific customers on whom to focus and those who drain money from the casinos. Similarly, Capital One tests tens of thousands of distinctive credit card offerings each year, using the latest technology and people to target the right offers to the right segments at the right time. These companies say that they know more about their customers than the customers do themselves. These in-house capabilities, once seen as the domain of the head of information technology or systems, arguably present an opportunity for Marketing and Information Technology to become one and the same.

6. Rationalizing the Brand Portfolio to Focus on Building Fewer, Stronger Brands

Leveraging Marketing's deeper understanding of the equities tied to each brand in the portfolio will help in sorting out which brands (or, more likely, names) the company should capitalize on, which should be built out, which should be migrated to other brands, and which should be eliminated altogether. In addition, the leading marketer will identify holes in the brand portfolio and suggest ways to fill them organically or through merger and acquisition efforts. A strong and smart brand portfolio has distinct roles set up for each brand, with clarity, differentiation, and customer value being the hallmarks.

This aspect of your strategic agenda must be handled with diplomacy since the brand portfolio can prove to be one of the most emotional, yet strategic issues on the table. To quote one of our client executives with brand portfolio responsibility, "Everyone with a dollar and a dream wants his/her own brand." Said another way, although it is relatively easy to create a brand, it is far more difficult for organizations to regularly and systematically review and invest (or divest) in their portfolios to determine whether they have the right mix of brands, maximizing customer and prospect value. As BP, UBS, Ingersoll Rand, Tyco, Emerson, Sara Lee, and Procter & Gamble know, companies can thrive if Marketing uses its insights to help their organization focus on fewer, more strategic, and powerful brands.

7. Simplifying and Coordinating the Selling Process

Giving the sales force more prescriptive selling tools—a deeper understanding of the segments and corresponding typing tools; a data-led customer relationship management warehouse of information about their customers; refreshed and revitalized value propositions tied to your major market offerings—will continue to help them be more effective. In addition, as Steve Meyer of Dell Services mentions, "You need to make sure that Marketing . . . is aligned with how your sales force is organized." The bottom line is that Marketing is on the hook for as many sales support tools as anyone else in the organization, from talking points and benefit drivers to segment-specific information—in other words, as a pharmaceutical sales rep puts it, the challenge of "what do I say when I only have the doctor's attention for thirty seconds?" Sean Burke states, "We once had a meeting of top sales and marketing employees in which we had the sales force critique every single piece of sales collateral created in the prior twelve months—rating each piece red, yellow, or green and explaining why. It was an incredibly eye-opening dialogue for both functions, but also demonstrated that the two functions depend on each other to ensure the organization's overall success."

In addition to helping simplify the selling process, Visionary Marketers should play a lead role in identifying and facilitating cross-selling opportunities across the enterprise, helping to realize synergies that most companies rarely achieve by developing a cross-pollinization mind-set across all business units. Beth Comstock sees this as one of her core roles as GE's CMO: "For a company like ours (multimarket, multibusiness), at the corporate level, you have to prioritize what is good for everyone and help to customize programs and tools for specific business units. We plant the seeds and give the businesses the coaching, tools, and understanding to create their own capabilities. We do try and employ a GE way of doing things, but still allow the practical nature of running separate businesses around the world to adapt the GE way to their specific needs."

Regarding cross-selling synergies, Shira Goodman has made a science of using the wealth of customer insights gathered from all Staples stores to drive cross-functional decision making, even in operations and merchandising. After five years, Goodman and her team get a lot of the credit for pushing Operations to use customer insights as a tool to drive sales and better levels of cutomer service.

8. Inspiring the Organization with a World-Class Market Strategy and Engagement Plan

While most consider this topic to be the CEO's job, it also provides another opportunity for Marketing to go well beyond the norm and own the job of galvanizing the employee base. Give employees a sense of purpose and aspiration, and customers will likely follow. Sean Burke, while in charge of marketing at GE Healthcare's Diagnostic Imaging (DI) Group, had been charged with not only reinventing (or reimagining) how DI goes to market—in a clear, distinct, customer-led, competitively advantaged way—but also to bring this new approach to twelve thousand employees to help carry the message externally. He worked with DI's CEO, Mark Vachon (now GE Healthcare President and CEO, Americas), to completely transform DI's product development and go-to-market approach, cutting across areas as diverse as product management, organizational design, training, and sales leadership. He was *given* this permission and license because he drove the discussion through a customer lens, incorporating this with GE's DNA. He took the opportunity to the organization because he views his role, and that of Marketing overall, to be growth drivers for the organization, not just marketing communications executors.

9. Managing the Innovation Pipeline as a True Portfolio

This is an area that every company seeks to upgrade by identifying white-space opportunities, capitalizing on unmet needs or underdeveloped categories, looking at the next generation of products and services and keeping its current portfolio fresh by identifying additional uses for existing products. As a senior marketer, you can drive the process of balancing risk and reward, as well as long-term and short-term needs, using customer insights as your secret innovation weapon.

For many companies where innovation does not have a natural home, marketing can credibly take on a leadership position because great innovation is ultimately insight led. Andy Stefanovich, founder of innovation consultancy PLAY (now a Prophet company), agrees. "Marketers should exist in the central and honorable position of driving the growth agenda at their company, tied to the inherent qualities of the topic: passion, seeing possibilities, driving insights and analysis, and encouraging risk taking, all at the core of any Visionary Marketer."

It is both the long- and short-term perspective and the ongoing assessment of opportunities, as well as the recognition that there will be innovation investments that have big payoffs and others that have smaller ones (or none at all), that makes innovation leadership more like managing an investment portfolio than simply monitoring a pipeline flow. In this type of scenario, the leadership that is necessary is that of the Visionary Marketer, who can bring business acumen as well as deep customer understanding to bear.

The concept of pervasive innovation is discussed in depth in the Third Shift.

10. Cultivating a Broad Internal and External Network

From an internal perspective, this means inspiring and motivating perhaps the most important source for new ideas that a company has at its disposal: its employee base. This means building networks within the organization to engage employees on the innovative ideas they have, as well as their ability and help in delivering the brand experience at the moment of truth.

American Express, Staples, and Best Buy use their internal networks on an ongoing basis. Jim Blann, former SVP Premium Value and Brand at American Express, noted that CEO Ken Chennault had set up an internal innovation fund and then encouraged all employees to submit proposals for innovation. All were evaluated and prioritized, and some eventually were funded. With two thousand stores globally, and fifteen hundred of those in the United States, Shira Goodman has a natural ongoing lab in which to try out new ideas and learn from the global employee base. And Barry Judge at Best Buy cannot overemphasize the importance of Blue Shirt Nation, an internal electronic bulletin board used by twenty-four thousand employees that senior executives scan daily to tap the pulse of employees' thoughts and comments on work policies. This internal source identifies insights and ideas tied to marketing, innovation, and the overall customer experience mix on an ongoing basis. Someone must orchestrate and assimilate all of these incredible sources of information, or a major asset will be underleveraged and opportunities possibly missed. This is a great role for Marketing to lead.

From an external perspective, senior marketers can make the most of the extended network of suppliers, vendors, and distribution partners to regularly tap into multiple sources of inspiration. Barry Krause, CEO of Innovation Consultancy Persuasion Arts and Sciences, keeps an open mind about innovation with his clients, such as Disney and Apple. He works with every external partner to bring in as many ideas as possible in a nonjudgmental way. Acura and W Hotels also see the value in working with external partners. They recently announced a marketing partnership under which Acura will be the preferred vehicle of W Hotels. W Hotels will feature the "Acura Experience," a chauffeured livery service offered as a benefit to hotel guests. The Acura Experience will be an extension of W Hotels branded "Whatever/Whenever" concierge services and will feature W Hotel amenities.

Overall, this *Network Effect*, which combines employees, partners, customers, and influencers, can be the single most important area where a marketer can have great impact, with potentially the highest profile, internally and externally.

The topic of more effectively leveraging your internal and external network will be discussed in the Second Shift.

11. Inspiring the Marketplace with a Galvanizing Platform and Big Idea: Targeting the Head and the Heart

From messaging to product and service delivery to customer service, to winning the battle for the dollar, growth-oriented marketers know that their first responsibility remains motivating and inspiring the marketplace to make a call to action on behalf of the brand. As Steve Jobs has accomplished with Apple, Howard Schultz with Starbucks, Richard Branson with Virgin, and Tony Hsieh at Zappos, combining world-class products and services with personal and authentic targeted messaging wins over fan bases, which inspires customers to use their voices to sell the brand as well.

Marketers with a growth agenda recognize that winning the hearts and minds of their customer base is also their job. Stephen Quinn believes that, at times, the simplest idea can cut through all of the noise and clutter in the marketplace and galvanize customers. "Save Money. Live Better" is a simple notion but a huge idea that instantly communicates the message that Walmart is devoted to bettering people's lives by offering world-class familiar brands at prices that allow them to save a little bit more than they can elsewhere, ultimately allowing them to have more money to spend on life's other needs. Communicating this type of functional and emotional benefit that could not be more relevant in today's environment is simple and personal—and brilliant. It is no wonder that the idea originated in a 1990 speech by one of the most brilliant retailers ever to walk the planet: Sam Walton.

12. Putting the Customer at the Center of the Universe

This sounds noble, grandiose, and a bit obvious, but too many companies put their capabilities at the center of their universe—"we make the best jet engines," "we produce the highest quality television shows," "we create the most cost-effective insurance policies"—instead of putting the customer in the center and discussing all of the different ways they can serve the customer. When Adam Stotsky was at the Sci-Fi Channel, he experienced a real "aha" moment when they took the TV out of the center of their conversations and put the target customer in the center. That small step allowed Sci-Fi to understand the essence of the brand, and with that insight, they could see many more ways of serving those customers: online, mobile, in theaters, in games. As a result, reaching aggressive growth aspirations did not seem so daunting. If the company had continued to center its conversation on the fall lineup while advertising revenues continued to plummet and production costs continued to rise, the Sci-Fi story may have turned out very differently from the success it is today.

The topic of relentlessly putting the customer at the center of your organizational efforts is discussed in depth in the Fifth Shift.

Owning the Right Strategic Imperatives

Once the marketer decides to seize an opportunity to become a strategic growth catalyst, it's important to determine which of the twelve growth topics will best showcase these catalytic capabilities across the organization, ultimately helping to achieve the company's longer-term growth objectives. To help prioritize potential initiatives, the marketer needs to do several things. First, he or she needs to see which of these growth topics should or could become corporate imperatives and then which Marketing can, and should, affect.

Second, the marketer must judge whether it can have this impact on an imperative directly or indirectly. For example, although marketing cannot singularly drive the decision to upgrade the organization's customer relationship management (CRM) system, the

Visionary Marketer will seize this opportunity to directly affect the specific type of customer data that Marketing can access through a new CRM system and thus the value of this investment. Actually, the Visionary Marketer will also see the CRM upgrade as a much needed tool to get closer to the customer through sophisticated data that will lead to better customer understanding and more intimacy. Clearly, Marketing is expected to lead the charge here.

Third, Marketing should have a plan for how best to accomplish the imperatives it carefully chooses to own: which activities, over what time frame, tied to what milestones, with which specific owners and metrics. Of course, the strategic imperatives that are traditionally marketing oriented will be easiest to accomplish, but they will also tend to keep Marketing somewhat insular from the rest of the organization. A portfolio of imperatives, including ones that Marketing can drive, co-own, or be part of is probably the best way to think about how a Visionary Marketer should go to market internally.

Your Five-Step Plan to Victory

Heads of Marketing who have led the strategy dialogue have generally followed a five-step path that starts with the simple notion that they are taking the organization on a journey over time, aimed at helping the executive team articulate the three- to five-year vision and its strategy. Importantly, the Visionary Marketer knows that this is not something accomplished in a two-day offsite meeting. Rather, it is an extended, informed, and aspirational conversation. Here are those steps.

Step 1: Get Alignment

Get alignment that this is something the organization can benefit from and that there is merit in embarking on this path. Smart CEOs may want to think more about their three- to five-year strategy, but in reality, they are tied to short-term quarterly pressures or have little experience in leading this type of dialogue or other priorities, so many never actually get to it. When they are approached on the topic, they may talk about revenue targets and expansion efforts but not specific strategies to get there.

If this is the case for your organization, the CEO will embrace the notion of engaging his or her team on the topic of long-term strategy and growth and will embrace the idea of someone else stepping up to lead the team through the process. Some marketers specifically ask for permission to lead, others hijack time set aside to review marketing to start the dialogue, and others take the organization through a Gantt chart type of process with milestones, activities, and responsibilities all outlined. Regardless of the spark, getting alignment on the importance of the dialogue and getting it started is the first step.

Step 2: Equip the C-Suite to Engage in the Dialogue in a Meaningful Way

Mark Gambill, CMO of CDW, a leading provider of technology products and services, had a vision that to really engage the leadership team at the level he wanted, he would have to plant seeds along the way. He would need to have frequent conversations, work sessions, and updates on the segmentation, positioning, and competitor analysis work he was leading, all the while knowing that certain executives in his organization would be able to truly participate in a longer-term discussion on strategy only if they were grounded in the facts first. He needed to address a slew of questions:

- Which segments of the market are we winning with today, and why?
- What types of customers are looking for an end-to-end technology solution rather than just a product?
- How big is the market opportunity?
- How are you defining the market opportunity?
- What brand equities do we own, aspire to own, can never own, and don't ever want to own?

The more upfront engagement, debate, and education you arm your peers with, the more fruitful the strategic dialogue down the road will be. Whether this is a six-week, six-month, or year-long process depends on the profile of your executive team, the relationships that exist at the C-level, and how ready these executives are to engage in the process.

Step 3: Start and Lead the Dialogue

It may seem obvious, but getting the dialogue going and truly leading the discussion of what the company can become is not as easy a topic to launch into as it first might appear to be. This dialogue will be somewhat informed by your current profile and all of the data with which you have carefully armed your executive team. But more than anything else, it depends on the integration and summation of the aspirations of the executive team and what they believe the organization can become.

Visionary Marketers always enter into the first "inspire and aspire" work session with questions:

- What do we want to be famous for five years from now?
- What is the headline of the *Fortune* magazine cover story about our company going to say?
- When we are selling our brand, products, services, and individuals five years from now, what are we actually selling?
- How will our frame of reference change (from products to services or services to solutions, for example)?

These are great thought stimulators to get the organization to start to hear what others believe is the future potential and to start to anchor the executives in what a vision of the future could be.

Once some degree of alignment is reached around whom the organization serves, what it should stand for, and how it thinks it can win, a pragmatic discussion has to take place about the current realities of the business. The competencies, competitive advantages, weaknesses, and the like have to be taken into account. Once they are thoroughly debated and thought through, you can enter into a broader version of the growth-gap discussion. In this case, the dialogue should be about bridging or closing the gap between your aspirational future state and the current realities.

Step 4: Lay Out the Strategies to Bridge the Gap Between Today and Tomorrow

At this point, you might want to turn to a few of the twelve growth topics. You might be getting hit with questions outside your traditional realm, such as operational continuous improvement, cross-functional integration and collaboration, information technology upgrades, and optimization of current assets. Nevertheless, even if the discussion is outside your normal range of expertise, you must be ready to engage in it at a C-suite level. In fact, only if you can become conversant across the entire range of strategic issues and across functions, geographies, businesses, products, and services will Marketing be able to sell itself as a strategic asset for the entire organization and a long-term partner for the CEO. Your ability to prioritize and balance specific growth initiatives and strategies outside your comfort zone, at the same time as you are handling traditional marketing responsibilities and toggle short- and long-term needs, will make this growth mind-set and organizational shift toward your place at the C-suite table a reality.

Step 5: Own the Imperatives

At first blush, this will seem highly administrative. Nevertheless, this step will keep you focused on *The Shift* over the long haul. Owning the list of strategic imperatives, along with the commensurate work plans, ownership, activities, milestones and metrics, and timing, while assisting each owner with his or her strategic imperative, will help the Visionary Marketer sustain a "shifted" position. The owners of the strategic initiatives will participate with the Visionary Marketer in an ongoing dialogue, built around quarterly updates, annual refreshes, and progress check-ins.

Keeping the Dialogue on Track

While getting the growth agenda started and moving from marketing to business strategy is important, sustaining the momentum of each imperative is equally as important.

Drive and Partner in Dialogue

As you think through these initiatives, remember that each represents a multifunctional bridge builder, allowing the Visionary Marketer to solicit, build, and nurture cross-functional C-suite relationships. Pick any one, and you will see some combination of Sales, Finance, Human Resources, R&D, or Information Technology playing a role in bringing the initiative to life. Pick any two or three initiatives, and you may possibly span the entire organization. All things being equal, you should attempt to engage in dialogues that span across as much of the organization as possible.

If you do not relentlessly drive and partner in the strategic dialogue across the executive team, keeping up a consistent rhythm and approach, time, effort, and good intentions will slip away—along with your credibility. Follow-through and leading by example are hallmarks of Visionary Marketers who understand that strategy is ongoing. It is easy to put strategy on hold while you try to meet the numbers, get a new product launched on time, or cut costs across the board. But if you co-own the growth agenda, it will be your job to keep executives' eyes on the strategic vision. Barry Judge, CMO of Best Buy, suggested that the CMO should make sure strategy is on the Board agenda each quarter to force a regular dialogue about strategic progress on an ongoing basis.

The Administrative Trap

Resist becoming trapped inside just an administrative role as you strive to lead a more strategic dialogue within your organization. As one CMO mentioned, "It is easy to get caught in becoming the administrative arm for all things strategic and actually forgetting to contribute to the strategic dialogue." Another CMO said:

> We have a group called the Strategic Initiatives Group that administers the strategic planning process, acting as an internal consulting group for various businesses. They determine different business opportunities we should consider pursuing. Over time, however, they end up facilitating the process and forget to bring strategic content to the dialogue. They have important titles, but they fail to lead us in an ongoing and thoughtful strategic dialogue, so our CEO ends up driving the discussion and singularly owning strategy.

This CMO vowed to change the pattern and step up to become the strategic voice and driver of the strategy going forward. She admits it will be an uphill battle, hampered by the way the organization has approached this in the past.

Don't Give Up Your Day Job

Don't forget to do your day job flawlessly. As Bob Harris mentioned earlier, "Credibility comes from execution. You cannot be perceived as only coming up with great strategy or only driving to great execution. You have to do both—always. The minute you lose sight of successfully delivering on your day-to-day responsibilities will be the minute you start to lose your audience."

Don't Bite Off Too Much

The most crucial mistake you can make is taking on too much strategy. Leaders of strategic dialogues and companies in general typically fail because they overcommit, overprioritize, lack focus, and don't put enough resources against any one strategic initiative to be successful. As Peter Senge wrote in *The Dance of Change*, start small, get some wins, and grow from there. Not only is fewer better, but those fewer need to be properly resourced and have hard metrics put against them to track the progress and return on investment on specific strategic initiatives over time.

The Dialogue Itself Will Change

Successfully making *The Shift* is about permanently changing the dialogue with your peers, the profile for Marketing, and the path to reaching your company's growth objectives. Making *The Shift* brings value to all functional areas while helping the organization clearly prioritize its opportunities for growth. Making *The Shift* allows senior marketers to focus on the bigger, transformational bets for their organization, while building a world-class marketing team to carry on the day-to-day tasks of traditional marketing roles and responsibilities.

So, What Do I Do on Monday Morning?

Making a successful shift from creating marketing strategies to driving business impact is the first shift in starting to change Marketing's position in your organization permanently. Without success here, Marketing will continue to be boxed in. With success here, new possibilities will start to open up for marketing.

1. Understand what your marketer profile is today—from tactician to visionary, what archetype your company most closely aligns to, and which success factors you do or do not have working in your favor to better understand the success formula to change your leadership profile from where it is today to becoming a Visionary Marketer.
2. Audit your success relative to the three critical Visionary Marketer components required to change the dialog from marketing as a function to marketing as an asset: your ability to leverage customer insights into in-market impact, your ability to show up with a P&L mind-set, whether you own a P&L or not, and your ability to earn credibility and trust across your peer set and in the executive suite.
3. Leverage the power of the insights at your fingertips to quickly start sharing insights and commensurate areas of impact with the executive team and other functional areas to start to spur

growth agenda topics. Embrace the notion that insights give you the power, confidence, and credibility that Marketing has so often lacked—not being the owner/repository of customer insights is a huge missed marketing leadership opportunity.

4. Discover your personal path to earning credibility and trust throughout the C-Suite, whether it is going in the field and "working the registers" or building strong alliances with the CFO.
5. Start every growth conversation with a business strategy/business impact lead in and not a marketing lead in—always in service of the articulated five year strategy.
6. Capture your CEO's imagination, by leading discussions tied to the five macro Wall Street/shareholder objectives he or she is always trying to achieve.
7. Have the courage to step up to lead the strategic growth discussion. Always link back to the macro Wall Street objectives and always with an eye on either acquisition, retention, or deepening share of wallet with customers and prospects.
8. Leverage any subset of the 12 Strategic Growth Topics to spur the dialog with the executive team, push in areas that you are not necessarily comfortable with, and form alliances with those that can help you achieve the objectives of the dialog.
9. Embark on The Five Step Plan to Victory, helping you to co-own the strategic growth agenda; avoid the administration trap.
10. Get going. Start small and recognize that you are on an impact journey. Pick parts of the strategy you want to personally own and others you want to simply have a voice on. Search for big and small strategic victories. You'll be surprised how early wins can begin to change the internal dialogue from creating marketing strategy to driving business impact.

The next four shifts are critical to completing the entire shift. Chapter Two proceeds to the Second Shift: from controlling the message to galvanizing your network.

2

THE SECOND SHIFT

From Controlling the Message to Galvanizing Your Network

Nike. So much comes to mind when you hear the word. You think athleticism. You think Air Jordan. You think *Just Do It*. You think about Phil Knight and his journey from being an avid runner to building the world's foremost athletic experience company in the world. "Athletic experience"? Not "shoe company"? Long ago, Nike stopped being only about the shoe and, to some degree, even about performance.

Interestingly, if you Google "Nike," you will see virtually no recent articles about new shoes being introduced or a new clothing line being launched or even a new spokesperson being signed. Instead you will see headlines and stories like these:

Nike, Google Kick Off Soccer Social-Networking Site

The sporting goods giant and the Internet search king have teamed up to create Joga.com and connect soccer fans around the world. [*BusinessWeek*, March 2006]

Nike 6.0 Goes Viral with Online Social Community on the Loop'D Network

Loop'd Network, the leading social network for action sports, today launched the Nike 6.0 online community to build a dedicated community to reach athletes and enthusiasts who are passionate about surf, snow, freeski, freeride, wake, moto and BMX. [Reuters, June 2008]

Nike 10K Human Race Largest Ever

Tens of thousands of runners around the globe, competing against other runners, other cities, all raising money for the World Wildlife Foundation, the Lance Armstrong Foundation and Sports for Refugees Camps. [Numerous publications worldwide, August 2008]

Nike Foundation and Buffetts Join to Invest $100 Million in Girls

The Nike Foundation and Peter and Jennifer Buffett, co-chairs of the NoVo Foundation, announced today an innovative collaboration to invest in "the girl effect": the ability of adolescent girls in developing countries to bring unprecedented social and economic change to their families, communities and countries. [*Nike News*, May 2008]

The New Advertising Outlet: Your Life

Steve Saenz used to run a 10K race in 36 minutes. But last spring—20 years, 2 children and 50 pounds later—he

> found himself seriously out of shape. A new website from Nike, he says, has brought him back on track. Since April, Mr. Saenz, 53, has been running with a Nike+, a small sensor in his running shoes that tracks his progress on an Apple iPod he carries. After each run near his home in Louisville, Ky., he docks the iPod into his computer and posts details of his run on the Nike+ website. There, he has made friends with other runners around the world who post running routes, meet up in the real world and encourage one another on the site . . . *a true support network.* [*New York Times*, October 2007]

These examples represent a dramatic transition from the advertising and product introduction mind-set that fueled companies like Nike for years. Each shows Nike building a global network, based on building connections in every pocket of the world, using sport and its products as its golden thread. And although the *New York Times* article may seem a bit more like traditional marketing and advertising, make no mistake. Trevor Edwards, Nike's Corporate Vice President for Global Brand and Category Management, states, "At the end of the day, Nike is not in the business of keeping media companies alive, we are in the business of connecting with consumers around the world."

Edwards's challenge is echoed by Michael Tchao, Product Director of Nike+:

> With Nike, you are no longer just buying a sneaker. You are joining the largest global running club. We offer you shoes and apparel that help you run longer and faster. This is our "hardware." We now offer you cool "software": ways to track your progress, tools to find people to challenge. We want to keep you active and motivated. . . . It's a very different way to connect with consumers.

> People are coming into this site, on average, three times a week and, thus, we do not have to go to them.

Nike's World's Largest 10K Run brings these points home. Of course, the 2008 Redeem Team Olympic Gold medalists, sponsored by Nike, helps. Yes, people want to be associated with Tiger Woods, and yes, every college athletic program is proud to have a swoosh on its jersey, but these are just a few of the many tactics that Visionary Marketers at Nike have at their disposal to build bonds with consumers that most likely were not attainable before.

If you think about what Phil Knight has created and what Edwards and Tchao bring to life every day, there are two key points. First, this is no longer about just effectively employing traditional advertising or just traditional marketing communication tactics (this is covered in depth in Chapter Four, the Fourth Shift). Second, and more important, their primary job today in driving the Nike brand forward is to build connections, bridges, and a living network with consumers around the world in ways that are most relevant to them, drive the business forward, and, yes, ultimately sell more shoes and athletic wear.

This Nike story is not unique. Starbucks has never really been simply about the coffee or Apple about the computer. These companies and brands have transcended product and function and are all about the identities they have built, the auras they have created, the bases of fans they have nourished over time, and the experiences customers have every time they interact with one of these brands.

Critical to these company's successes has been the fact that all have spent an inordinate amount of time building their companies and brands through an expanding network of users, influencers, social communities, bloggers, media, multichannels, and even disparagers. They long ago realized that there was just so much they could do to build and control their brand and that at some point, they had to turn their brands over to others, outside the company, to build it successfully in what we call the Network Era.

The Network Era

The Network Era is the third era in modern marketing. The first marketing era, often referred to as the golden age of advertising, was a world of one-way communications: marketers were in total control of the message and the vehicles to leverage. This first marketing era, following World War II, was the beginning of brand building and the rise of mass communications as the major driver of sales. Mass, one-way communication in the form of TV, print and radio advertising, and sponsorships were the hallmarks of this era, which lasted until the mid-1990s. At that time a shift occurred with the Internet ushering in the second marketing era, allowing two-way communications, solicitation of input and feedback from customers to improve the offer, and a new approach to building loyalty across key, profitable segments.

During the current, third marketing era, two-way communication has expanded among an exploding number of stakeholders as shown in Figure 2.1. This Network Era can be defined by the confluence of five core dynamics:

- An explosion in not just the number of, but also the power, and increasing influence of a myriad of stakeholder types.
- The novel and rapidly exploding innovation and introduction of thousands of new communication and interaction mechanisms to influence purchase behaviors.
- The increasing impact of the coalition activity of multiple networks, which are able to build, define, or tear down new markets.
- Citizen Marketing. Leveraging the network to unleash the full power of the consumer as marketer, whereby individuals create and participate in marketing campaigns for their favorite products, becoming loyal word-of-mouth advocates (or detractors).

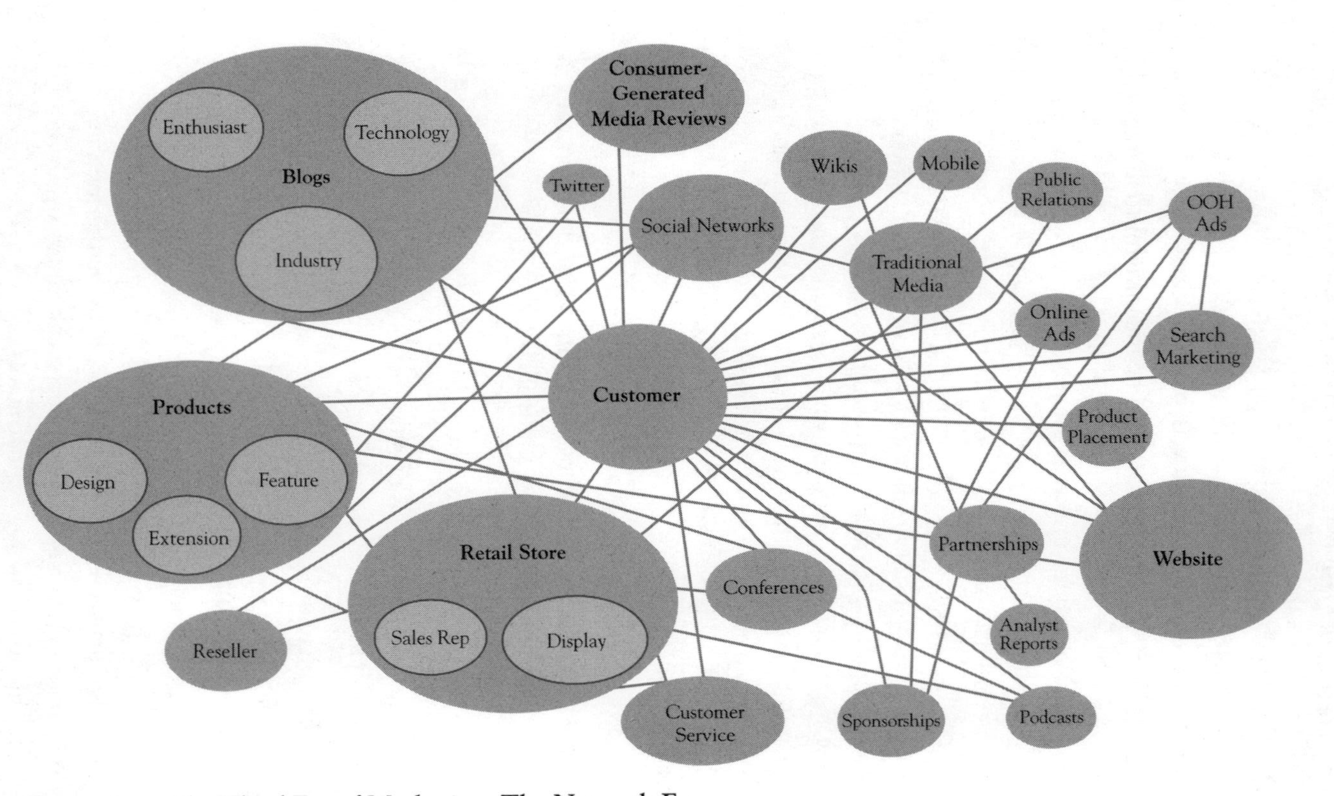

Figure 2.1 The Third Era of Marketing: The Network Era

- An increasing openness and transparency in a two-way manner—about consumers, their lives, their patterns of behavior, and their spending habits, as well as how a company goes to market. A corollary to this point is the increasing willingness of consumers to share personal information, which can be meaningful to marketers, in exchange for small perks, first-to-know status, or simply "no fee" use.

These do not represent the set of dynamics with which many marketers and traditional marketing companies grew up. As a result, marketers and business leaders now face the overwhelming task of integrating the implications of these dynamics into the company's overall corporate strategy, rather than solely its marketing or brand strategy.

To fully embrace these dynamics, it remains important to continue to remember that the underlying purpose of marketing for the Visionary Marketer and its intended impact remain the same as in the first two eras: getting products and services into customers' hands as effectively, efficiently, and profitably as possible. Although the dynamics have changed throughout the eras, the end game has not.

What has changed in each era, though, and what drives the new strategies of the Network Era is how companies most effectively and efficiently close the sale and build loyalty given these newer dynamics. Beth Comstock, CMO of GE, stated, "You can look at this new, networked, and hypercompetitive world in many different ways. We choose to see it as an incredible opportunity to reach our customers and all of the influencers surrounding them, from Wall Street to our employee base, in new and more powerful ways than ever before."

Thriving in the Network Era

Becky Saeger of Charles Schwab has internalized the reality of this Network Era and the key piece of this reality: that most brand managers and marketers have never really been in control of their brands. She has more easily come to terms with the new rules of the Network Era because she feels marketers suffered from an "illusion . . . that we ever believed we controlled the brand. It has always been in the control of customers." So how do *you* start to get your head and hands around how best to tackle managing the network opportunity for your organization, knowing it is not optional, as Saeger alludes to?

As you begin to understand your network and the strategic opportunity it can provide your company, start by being clear on what your company is trying to achieve strategically, how your company makes money, how your company gets the greatest number of valuable customers interested in your brand, and, most important, which elements of the marketing strategy and the brand network you can control and which you can only influence. This information is a necessary starting point for considering the opportunities associated with your company's network.

Furthermore, you need to recognize the context of the networked world in which brands and organizations operate, tied to the four critical Network Era success principles:

1. *From control to influence*. In the past, Marketing was all about trying to control every interaction or touch point. In the networked world, marketers have to recognize it is impossible to control everything. At best, they can hope to influence key stakeholders and facilitate the right kind of experience.
2. *From push to pull*. In a customer-centric world, customers are telling companies what they want and don't want from their company of choice. The days of companies telling customers what they are going to get are over.
3. *From communication to engagement and participation*. In the networked world, brands need to engage stakeholders with information, activities, and services that add value, as well as participate in the conversation and experience.

4. *From closed to open, transparent, and authentic.* In a digitally driven world, all information makes its way to the web, where brands are identified for bad products, practices, or services. The best strategy is to be open, honest, and authentic from the start and let the network do much of the heavy lifting.

Let's examine these four Network Era success principles in greater detail.

From Control to Influence and from Push to Pull

Part of enjoying the same success that companies like Apple, Nike, and Starbucks have experienced in this networked world includes giving up the command and control of your brand in a nonnegotiable way. This is a hard concept to grasp because in the past, brand managers' control over the brand was sacred ground. By controlling the message and the delivery vehicles, traditional marketers were able to push the right customers to the right channels, having them pay the right price for the right offerings, all in a very tidy way.

More progressive companies in the old days, particularly in the second era, learned that by focusing on the customer experience and engaging in an ongoing dialogue with customers, they could more readily launch new programs into the marketplace that were already vetted—a precursor to the open innovation and co-creation concepts that are discussed in the Third Shift in Chapter Three. Companies like Southwest Airlines and Saturn proved you could integrate the customer into the business and still drive profitable growth and increases in brand equity. They developed strong brands by managing and controlling their touch points, emphasizing the total customer relationship, and optimizing activities across every point of interaction, while still controlling the relationship.

In today's Network Era, the exponential proliferation of touch points seems to have caused a total disruption to business as usual. Yet it is important to remember that a brand exists in the mind of the customer, and in that sense, it has never really been the exclusive property of the company. Fundamentally, a brand is a tangible assignment of value to the relationship between company and consumer. This being true, there is no reason the company has to maintain sole control or fear losing control. In fact, ceding some of that control to customers has always been part of truly successful brand building.

Still, although it is easy to talk about marketers' giving up control, it is hard for many of them to do so, a key separation point between Tactician Marketers and Visionary Marketers. Many companies have difficulty understanding that ceding some elements of control is more likely to spur growth and loyalty, not chaos.

Others, like Adobe, have found that by opening up their processes to allow those in the brand network to have a voice has engendered greater and stronger loyalty. Adobe, discussed in more detail in the Third Shift, uses its website as the focal point of building and extending its brand. Ann Lewnes, Senior Vice President of Corporate Marketing at Adobe, believes, "The loyalty engendered toward Adobe has increased because our customers and prospects feel like they are able to shape our offerings." Adobe has profited from being more open to its constituents. Lewnes continues:

> We have very active users in our communities and third party bloggers who get a lot of access to Adobe; we are truly networked. We also have our own bloggers who are empowered to write about our products and technologies. We had to hand over control. It is a powerful way to have people feel a part of the brand.

Although it may be difficult to accept this new paradigm, it is nonetheless impossible to ignore. And like Adobe, more and more companies have found that giving up control can be good for business. For instance, eBay and Google provide tools that allow their customers to create the type of relationship they want to have with the company, not the other way around. They enable, rather than dictate, behavior. As a secondary benefit, new businesses are created to meet the needs that the new customer behaviors have created. By basing their value proposition on the release of control, they have flourished and drawn their customers in as next-generation sources of innovation and, de facto, advocacy.

Whom Does the Networked Customer Trust?

Given the 24/7 nature of online communications, stakeholders converse with each other long after the brand manager goes home and far earlier than he or she arrives at work in the morning. Tightly focused groups of constituents interact on the topics they care about, with ever-increasing influence. As a result, Visionary Marketers have to manage their brands as networks, hoping at best to play a major influencing role in the dialogue. The optimistic way of looking at this ongoing dialogue is that never before have marketers or executives across an enterprise had such an open window into truly understanding their customers. They can hear unfiltered customer feedback in its purest form—right from the keyboard and not from the traditional one-way mirrored room, which often induces forced and unnatural comments.

Josh Bernoff, an analyst at Forrester Research and coauthor of *Groundswell*, says, "We're in a world where one person, by their actions, can make a company look bad, and it can get echoed and amplified over and over again. The power has shifted, [so] that big companies now have to be worried about one individual with a microphone called a blog."

Companies fully engaged in the Network Era recognize that they will have to take control of a few critical "moments of truth" that they cannot afford to lose control of. Zappos, the online clothing and shoe retailer, made a strategic choice not to outsource customer service in order to be positioned as an online service leader. CEO Tony Hsieh believes customer service is one of the most critical touch points in the network and invests heavily in training in-house customer service representatives to provide the best possible service. In fact, most Zappos employees work on the front lines in positions that directly affect the customer experience. Unlike other companies, Zappos puts its 800 number front and center on its Web site, because, as Hsieh explains, "We want people to call us. That's when you get five to ten minutes of someone's undivided attention and an opportunity to talk to them. This is how to make the 'message' and Zappos' brand promise stand out." This is a great example of how companies can gain customer trust in the network era.

Understanding the variety of stakeholder groups or touch points that may be influencing your product or brand is a critical piece of the loss-of-control equation. So is recognizing the myriad of vehicles that are being used, with or without your permission, to talk about you, your company, your brand, your employees, your service, and your offerings. As Jonah Bloom of *Advertising Age* states, "The truth is that consumers trust fellow buyers before they do marketers." Because this is the new reality and customers are already moving rapidly into the Network Era, marketers face pressure to change.

Becky Saeger at Schwab can relate with personal experience: "We had to come to grips that an investor might trust the opinion of an anonymous user in a stock web group more than our own investment management professionals. And that was a hard pill to swallow."

Visionary Marketers are recognizing that they no longer have total control and are starting to determine what discussions they can influence, especially when others talk about their brands in forums like these:

- Category-specific blogs like Gizmodo (for technology/gadget lovers) or FlyerTalk (for frequent flyers)
- User-generated reviews from online retailers like Amazon
- Opinions posted from segment-specific, yet not industry-specific, affinity groups and the ability of these blogs to

have dramatic impact, positive or negative (for example, mom-oriented blogs such as momsbuzz.com)

- Unbiased industry-content aggregators like CNET
- Unbiased satisfaction and quality rankings—from J. D. Power to *Consumer Reports*
- Social networking sites, such as Facebook, Ning, and MySpace
- 24/7 text messaging (like Twitter) and 24/7 cable commentators (like CNN)

With all of these stakeholders to influence and vehicles to deliver the message, it is increasingly likely that customers will no longer go to the company website or sales force for product information. They believe they can get much better information and make a much more informed purchase decision by getting answers from others, not you, to questions such as these:

- What is the actual price, and how do I negotiate my way into getting it?
- How is this product truly better than others I might consider?
- What are the problems others have encountered with the product?
- How does the company deliver customer service?
- Which retailers should I avoid?
- How does all of this change if I go to one of the competitors?

In effect, these stakeholders are stating that they trust other sources first, before they will trust you as an objective source when it comes to answering these questions.

This may be even more important in a business-to-business environment. No longer does the customer have to wonder helplessly, *Should I trust the salesperson, or is he just working for the company, not me?* Instead today's buyers can be fully informed in terms of their most critical purchase drivers. A business-to-business brand network, which may include industry white papers, engineer user groups, and advocacy groups, has as much of an impact on whether a sale gets made as does the salesperson with a hearty handshake and detailed product feature sheets.

Visionary Marketers understand the power that resides in their brand network's complex influence patterns. They pick and choose how and where to best engage with an expanding set of interested stakeholders. They know that success can be had in this hyper-networked world if they focus on touch points they can control directly, influence those who can be influenced indirectly, and respond to those who may be out of their sphere of influence and control but can harm them if left unattended. No response is still a response. They also know that providing an open and transparent dialogue on their product, service, features, benefits, support, and pricing will be standard operating procedure going forward, because the customer will come to the table with that information regardless of the source. Why not start building trust from day one and become *the source*?

Car Buying Is Now Child's Play

Consider how the network has dramatically shifted the way in which customers enter the process of buying a car. Customers now painstakingly research the makes and models they are interested in on cars.com and Edmunds.com, which has accurate up-to-the-minute pricing for their local area. They can download mini-applications that allow them to understand the inventory of particular models within a hundred miles of their dealership. They can access dozens of user groups, in which the forums provide user experience: what works well, what breaks easily, which dealers give great service (or do not), warranty issues, aftermarket modification possibilities, and more. J. D. Power and *Consumer Reports* almost seem as if they were designed for the rookie league, with the amount of information available today, as does the sales rep in the dealer showroom.

Although the manufacturer still controls the showroom and how it trains its salespeople, and ultimately the ease of the process of buying a vehicle, the days of "let me see if my manager will let me give you that price" are over. As a result, extending out from the dealer experience are hundreds of potential network touch points—blogs, user groups, videos, Facebook groups, car buying services—that will either help or hurt the company in closing the deal. Importantly, many of these touch points will likely be connected to key touch points that the company does control, such as advertising, promotions, and after-sales service, which in effect allow a company to work backward on how it should control certain aspects of the experience.

From Communication to Engagement and Participation

Taking advantage of the brand network requires a revolution in the interactions between various parts of the business and major changes in the roles that marketers play to take strategic advantage of interactions. By actively participating in, engaging with, and thus influencing the networks, Visionary Marketers should be able to tap directly into a valuable resource that:

- Provides them with a potential army of advocates, helping to sell their offerings in both objective and authentic ways.
- Serves as a key source for innovation and new ideas by clarifying what is of particular interest to the members

of the network and better identifying the network needs against which their current offer does not deliver. This encourages rapid feedback for new products and services.

- Identifies gaps in the customer experience and provides the best mechanism to rapidly deliver remarkable customer service to fill those gaps in a highly targeted fashion.
- Gives insight into permission barriers. In the past, companies entered new categories or adjacent markets with the best tools available: great offers and sound market research. However, only the brand network can provide the level of insight into why the company may or may not be accepted for its new strategy.
- Provides insight into customer needs and current levels of satisfaction with the company and its competitors. This also provides insight into causality around why certain behaviors are occurring, what drives key outcomes, and who is most important to the success of the business.
- Identifies new partnering opportunities. The network can teach you which other brands it respects. As important, customers can lead you to the partnerships they have formed, using your products and services in conjunction with those of other companies.

In his dramatic return to the helm at Starbucks in 2008, Howard Schultz took this concept to heart. Although it is still early in his second watch and he is operating within a greatly constrained financial environment, Schultz has recently launched the first Starbucks loyalty program, Starbucks Gold Rewards, through its recently built participative network, mystarbucksidea.com. Through mystarbucksidea, ideas like loyalty cards, new offerings, and new potential partnerships are surfaced, voted on, and considered for use in new go-to-market offerings. Starbucks even states on its mystarbucksidea page:

> You know better than anyone else what you want from Starbucks. So tell us. What's your Starbucks Idea? Revolutionary or simple—we want to hear it. Share your ideas, tell us what you think of other people's ideas and join the discussion. We're here, and we're ready to make ideas happen. Let's get started.

This has not always been the case at Starbucks. While delivering a world-class customer experience has been the foundation of the company, actively engaging consumers in an ongoing dialogue and acting on their ideas was not the operating norm. If it was, the loyalty program would have been developed a decade ago. However, to fully engage and participate, you have to be willing to shift old behaviors.

As you might suspect from this test, as well as the earlier Nike example, billions of dollars are being reallocated from traditional advertising budgets aimed at talking to customers, to budgets aimed at building networked brands, engaged communities, and enduring relationships through a fully active and participative approach. And although not everyone has as sophisticated and holistic a network approach as Nike or Starbucks does, many are finding successes in their own way.

Carolyn Groobey, former Head of Consumer Strategy at Bill Me Later and now a marketing executive at PayPal, part of eBay, used her brand network to engage with her consumers. She describes this shift:

> What has happened is that you always had people talking about your brand, but you didn't have a window into the actual start of the dialogue. But now, with the brand network, you can listen to the dialogue, determine how to use that information to better build the business

> and also, ultimately, figure out how to influence the dialogue—that is where we are at today.

To this point, Rory Finlay, the CMO of Jim Beam Brands, is shifting the major emphasis of his multimillion-dollar marketing budget away from advertising toward "fanning the flames of word of mouth [more] than anything else." For this reason, Jim Beam Brands is changing its entire marketing approach, which is now aimed at creating a dynamic brand and network, helping to build and sell its brands, ultimately in a more genuine, authentic, and substantive way, through the power of the consumer.

Importance of Engagement and Participation

Clearly, these Visionary Marketers are adopting new strategies and tactics to capitalize on their brand networks more effectively. They recognize that customers and interested stakeholders have tens of thousands of forums and venues in which to share their opinions in one-to-one and one-to-many ways. And as you can imagine, the importance of these brand network dynamics mushrooms with every subsequent technological advancement.

How important is the engagement and participation aspect of *The Shift*? The interest in brand networks has pushed Procter & Gamble to alter its proven approaches to testing and building awareness around some of its most critical product line extensions, tied to its billion-dollar brands, by relying heavily on word-of-mouth and buzz marketing and relatively little on mass media. This is the case for the launch of Crest Weekly Clean Intensive Cleaning Paste. To introduce the product, P&G sent new product samples through its 600,000-strong Vocalpoint "buzz Marketing program for moms." As expected, many of the mothers used Twitter to convey their interest in the product, and P&G followed up the sample release with a survey to identify how to modify the product. Expectations are high that this will be another blockbuster line extension, and Crest, one of P&G's biggest-spending media brands (with almost $250 million in annual measure media spending), is relying on a network to drive its success. Clearly this is not the traditional intensive sales force and promotional push approach.

Galvanizing the Network: Obama Style

President Barack Obama understood the importance of participation and engagement. It's no secret that his historic and highly strategic campaign, based on networked grassroots organizing efforts, drove him straight to the White House. What lies beneath the myriad of articles on the subject is the core theme in *The Shift.* Obama and his team transformed the campaign and election process with the use of new media and communication strategies to promote individual engagement and record voter-level participation in the political process. He largely bypassed the issues of ethnicity, race, and experience and instead focused on bringing voters into the dialogue, which was largely shaped by voters. Obama's victory was a calling card to all Visionary Marketers: innovation, engagement, and participation are critical to winning over new customers and further entrenching current ones. Here are a few steps that Obama's campaign took, which Visionary Marketers can learn from:

Change You Can Believe In The first step in Obama's strategy was to build a strong positioning platform for all communication and strategic agenda efforts. While his opponent chose to emphasize experience, Obama focused his platform on a message of change—change from the current administration and change from the mistake-ridden past. Beyond political change, this approach also signaled a new method for communication and supporter engagement.

The Obama campaign launched initiatives to garner wide-ranging support from voters across demographics. Peter Field, in "What Obama Can Teach You," noted that among the young voter segment, his strategists used applications such as the Apple iPhone application, "Countdown to Change," to not only increase awareness of his agenda but also to drive young voters, a valuable and yet difficult group to motivate to the polls. In addition, the Obama campaign both recognized and acted on key statistics showing a tremendous amount of growth in Internet use for news and politics. According to Andrew Raseij and Micah Sifry, a study by the Pew Research center conducted from 2004 to 2008, showed the percentage of Americans who said the Internet was their main source of political news was up 33% from 10% in 2004.

From Old School to MyBo In early 2007, the Obama campaign hired Chris Hughes, one of the founders of Facebook.com, to build a social networking website nicknamed MyBo. This site, inspired by other successful social networking websites such as myspace.com and facebook.com, later transformed into www.my.barackobama .com, where supporters could "join local groups, create events, sign up for updates and set up personal fund-raising pages," wrote Brian Stelter in "The Facebooker Who Friended Obama." The idea behind the development of this website came from Obama himself. Peter Field quoted him as stating, "One of my fundamental beliefs from my days as a community organizer is that real change comes from the bottom up, and there's no more powerful tool for grass-roots organizing than the Internet." The site was an enormous success; its strategy was so well coordinated, noted Jeanne Cummings in "Obama, the Billion-Dollar Man," that on the day of its launch, a thousand grass-roots groups appeared in Iowa, New Hampshire, Idaho, Virginia and other state locations. Obama also heralded a new generation of political activists who easily could reach out to constituents and undecided voters while pulling information such as e-mail addresses and phone lists, and organizing local fundraising events in short order.

The website and a substantial online phone database were used to mobilize efforts across the country. Supporters used tools on the Internet to create "Unite for Change" house parties to maintain Clinton's support base, once she dropped out of the race. Obama's supporters also used the site to organize support for Obama well before his campaign staff even arrived to work on that particular state's primaries. Infrastructure was created, and without massive campaign staff oversight, by willing and engaged participants. Voters became part of the political process rather than acting as bystanders, as they had in years past. With their efforts directly driving the campaign's success, supporters felt as though they owned this process (and the brand) as much as Obama himself did. In other words, this campaign transcended Barack Obama, becoming a personal and networked effort and investment for all American voters. This emotive trigger became the force for change in America.

Sealing the Deal Obama's staff recognized the campaign's independent strength and the fact that it did not require complete message control. They allowed supporters and donors to take control of parts of his campaign. Brian Stelter noted, "Fundraisers—both big and small—and other backers were given the freedom to organize their own events, operate their own blogs and engage in other activities that gave them a deeper sense of being part of the campaign." This strategy changed the dynamic of political campaigns from push/passive to pull/active. The level of volunteer engagement was staggering in comparison to that in the McCain campaign.

Obama team members were relentless in their tactics, using social networks to push their candidate's agenda as a call to action for all citizens. His was a message of engagement and participation in which he used new media networks as the tool to provide a means of action for his supporters. In the spring of 2008, members of Obama's team used his first-quarter fundraising success to provide support and tools for his supporters. They used training seminars for online activists and provided DVDs and other material for a national voter canvassing day. These actions signaled the seriousness and inclusiveness that Obama's campaign held for these organizers. The message was more about individual contribution to change than fundraising, according to Jeanne Cummings of Politico.com.

President Obama was recently named *Advertising Age's* 2008 Marketer of the Year and *Time's* Person of the Year for 2008, and, to most marketers, brand of year. Arguably, none of this could have happened had he and his team not fully embraced the power residing in the Network Era. The breadth of Obama's network is visualized in Figure 2.2 and can be organized in three distinct stages: pre-election, election, and post-election.

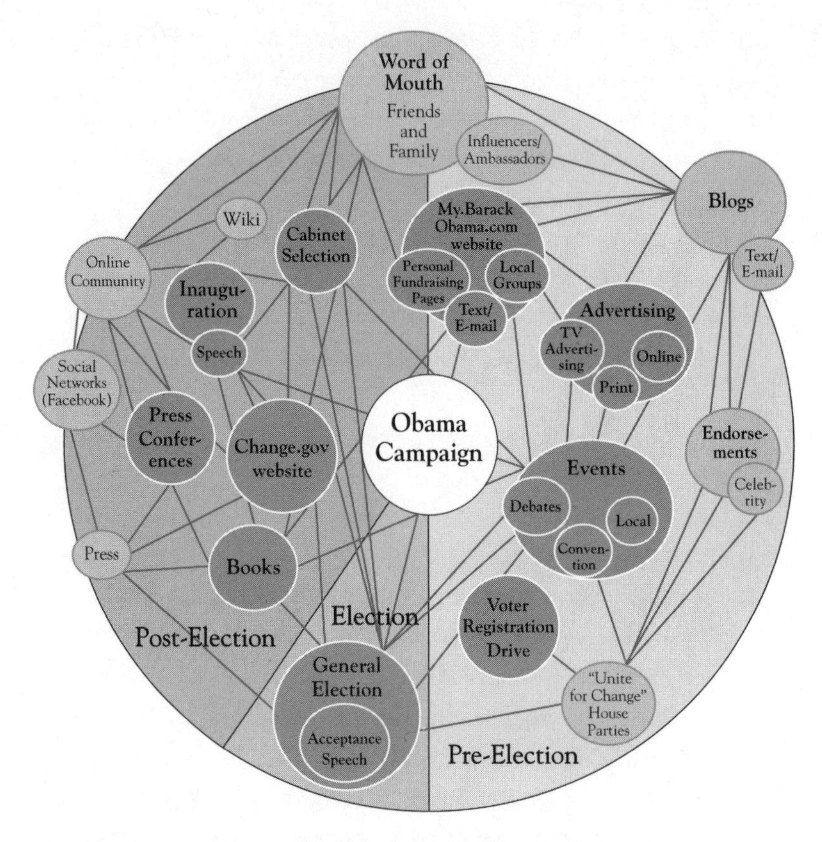

Figure 2.2 Example of Barack Obama's Touch Points

From Closed to Open, Transparent, and Authentic

This last point is a by-product of the previous three key points made in the Network Era success principles. The reality is that your businesses and brands are already open and transparent through consumer will; the choice of whether to embrace this reality and become an authentic brand is yours to make. Every company has a brand. Whether they choose to manage it in a proactive way is the question begging for an answer. We contend that this is the ultimate job of the Visionary Marketer: to build your brand, in a way that is true to who you are or aspire to become.

From GE to Coca-Cola, Boeing to Nike, Schwab to Starbucks, companies have stressed the fundamental importance of authenticity to the brand's success. Successfully navigating in the Network Era will shape whether a brand can become, stay, or regain its relevance and authenticity.

Archetype I leaders continue to come back into their organizations to try and reinstill some of the core values that made their companies great in the first place. From Ralph Lauren to Howard Schultz, they recognize that the game has changed in terms of external stakeholder influences on customer purchase decisions, as has the need to balance reinvention with authenticity.

When Howard Schultz worked out the details of his revitalization effort for Starbucks, he outlined four initiatives to restore the luster of this iconic brand. Schultz described one of the initiatives as

> reigniting our emotional attachment with our customers by restoring the connection our customers have with you, our coffee, our brand, and our stores. Unlike many other places that sell coffee, Starbucks built the equity of our brand through the *Starbucks Experience*. It comes to life every day in the relationship our people have with our customers. By focusing again on the *Starbucks Experience*, we will create a renewed level of meaningful differentiation and separation in the market between us and others who are attempting to sell coffee.

McDonald's is a great example of a brand that struggled for years to regain its past glory and ultimately found its way back to its roots, capped through the "I'm Lovin' It" campaign. In 2003, the company initiated a dynamic revitalization strategy that has won back customers and generated strong revenue and profit growth. Marketing helped lead the way by rebalancing the company's product portfolio, retooling its positioning, and strengthening its massive integrated marketing program. Through Visionary Marketer Mary Dillon, McDonald's has regained its focus on families, fully embraced the digital world, continues to add menu items—both healthier and more traditional—and has redesigned its look and feel to be more progressive, but stay true to its roots of offering good food at a good value in a fun environment. Not surprisingly, McDonald's is performing extremely well in a sullen economy and has had its brand rise in the most recent *BusinessWeek/Interbrand* Best Global Brands study, ranking as the eighth most valuable brand in the world.

Comcast, in contrast, has been forced to think more about its own authenticity and recognized the need to develop an authentic voice within the much maligned telecom world. To most, Comcast is seen as a big cable conglomerate and viewed by customers with all the frustration accorded a monopoly. It has a reputation for poor customer service, which has gotten a lot of play on the "I hate Comcast" blogs. Comcast has taken this discontent to heart and is attempting to take some positive steps toward building authenticity in an online environment where it has not been in control. Although there are still "I hate Comcast postings" in the blogosphere, Comcast also has ComcastCares on Twitter, where Frank Eliason, a digital care manager, is working to respond to Comcast customer issues or problems, usually within twenty-four hours. Comcast may have a long way to go to become a truly powerful and authentic brand, but one man's actions can go a long way to establishing the trust-based relationships most brands and marketers yearn for.

The Dell example on the following page brings the four network era success principles to life.

Network Touch Points

The trick in fully realizing the benefits of a networked approach is to understand the dynamics of how your brand interacts with your customers in both apparent and not-so-apparent ways. This is where the concept of understanding how all of the touch points surrounding your brand come into play.

The Network Era and Dell

Nowhere have the four Network Era success principles been more evident than in how Dell has transformed its go-to-market approach and brand by increasing its ability to participate in and influence its networked environment.

Dell has come a long way from 2005 when Jeff Jarvis infamously went on his Dell Hell crusade and almost single-handedly did more damage to the Dell brand, through his blog, than any three years of good advertising work could do on the positive side. Today, Jarvis admits Dell has come full circle, stating, "We ended up agreeing, and they ended up seeing the value in listening to and ceding control to customers. They reached out to bloggers; they blogged; they found ways to listen to and follow the advice of their customers. They joined the conversation."

Dell is not just participating in the networked environment and economy; it is using it to dramatically improve its performance. Dell's leadership is now tirelessly focused on leveraging the brand network to its fullest extent. Mark Jarvis, Dell's former CMO, brought this point home in a 2008 keynote address:

> Don't transmit, but participate . . . let other people rate and review your products. At Dell.com, we set up ratings and review pages showing all of the reviews that we've had from various sources, from . . . consumers to professionals, which allows people to go look at what other people prefer. . . . This drives product sales. We have our own blog, which we call Direct to Dell, in which we basically publish information about things that we're doing. If there is a challenge—for example, you may remember the battery issue that we had—we were instantly on the blog, explaining the issue. By reaching out and participating and communicating with our customers, we were able to offset a lot of the negative potential issues associated with that battery issue. As Michael

> Dell recently stated, "I'd rather have [a negative] conversation in my living room [i.e., Dell.com] than in somebody else's."
>
> Also, you need to listen to your customers. About a year and a half ago, we set up a website called Idea Storm. And the idea was very simple: Tell us what you want. . . . A great example of this was about a year ago, when we had a whole bunch of people say, "We want Linux, the operating system, on our PCs." About 130,000 people said, "We want Linux." So we rapidly went and built a Linux PC and delivered it to the market about three months later. Incredible exposure, and we didn't do any marketing for it, because customers pulled us into it—it was their idea. Zero marketing dollars—what an incredible way of doing marketing!

Dell is doing more than making sure it is up on its social networking presence. It has about 5 million conversations with its customers either online or on the phones or in person every day, it has a customer database with about 58 million customers in it, and it has twelve thousand reports a day pulled out of that database in order to do various things for its twenty thousand daily active users worldwide. This all helps to drive Dell's successful $16 billion of online business, which is larger than Amazon.com and eBay.

Every part of Dell's go-to-market approach today can be traced directly back to the internal and external networks it has built. It has deliberately brought the customer into the dialogue. It is possibly ceding some dialogue and brand control, but is now able to make smarter market decisions, with much more confidence, because customers have told them what they specifically want and don't want from Dell. Dell has stopped talking at customers (or transmitting to them) and now talks with them.

A recent *Fortune* article by Anne Fisher commended Dell on its networked approach and identified it as an emerging best-in-class example of fully using its network to drive the business forward.

The network idea is so vastly different from the way marketers have traditionally thought about attracting and retaining customers that it can be simultaneously disorienting and overwhelming. Historically, most companies have followed a fairly linear approach to thinking through customer acquisition, generally starting with generating awareness, followed by getting into the consideration set, next being preferred over other choices, then having customers make the actual purchase, and then moving these customers into a long-term, loyalty-driven relationship. In a networked world, the end result is exactly the same—purchase and loyalty—but the path to that result is quite different.

A networked world has a host of active and participating touch points—significant, definable points of influence—ranging from a powerful individual's opinion to a specific collective stakeholder or user group's recommendation to traditional marketing tactics like partnerships or sponsorships. The challenge now is that these touch points can come from anywhere, credible or not, and in today's hyperconnected environment, they can determine the fate or success of a new feature, benefit, product offering, brand, or business, literally in seconds. A network of touch points that is managed and influenced (not controlled) well and deliberately can truly do a lot of the work in building a brand.

Understanding the Complete Network of Stakeholders

This explosion of stakeholder touch points and interaction points includes three distinct yet interrelated groups: those directly involved in value delivery, those influencing the purchase decision, and those who shape the market context (Table 2.1). What stands out in this list is the growing importance of employees in the Network Era. This key stakeholder group has the power to build the brand through their actions as corporate employees *and* their interactions, as your sales force, to all people they interact with, inside and outside your company. Best Buy's Blue Shirt Nation, a digital forum where employees talk to each other to share stories and tap

Table 2.1 Prominent Stakeholder Touch Points

Those Directly Involved in Value Delivery	Those Directly Influencing the Purchase Decision	Those Shaping the Market Context
Customers Consumers Channel partners and their channel partners Suppliers Aftermarket players Employees	Official media Blogs User groups Content aggregators and experts Affinity groups Employees	Industry analysts Wall Street Coalition partners Advocacy group Government Regulators

into insights that will ultimately help improve Customer Service and Marketing within Best Buy's stores, is an effective example of leveraging the power of this key stakeholder group.

The major challenge for marketers is not the sheer number of stakeholder types, because marketers can create two-way relationships with each. Instead, the challenge lies in managing the complex interaction of stakeholders with one another. In fact, Visionary Marketers have learned that the collective dialogue among stakeholders can yield insights that may be more important than anything else the company might discover.

Mapping Your Network of Touch Points

If you buy into the guiding principles, the next logical step is to better understand how you should approach the network question for your company, given your unique industry, category dynamics, and marketing history.

Every Visionary Marketer, like those at Adobe, Nike, and Apple, has learned that managing the brand network has to begin with a better understanding of how his or her own brand network has been and is being built. Because multiple stakeholders are involved in each transaction, each can play a beneficial or a detracting role, depending on their interactions with the company.

Thus, it is critical to go through a full network segmentation to truly understand the world your company and brand lives in. My previous book, *Building a Brand-Driven Business*, details a full touch point analysis methodology. Those principles still hold, yet now marketers must contend with the exponential growth of influencing (and increasingly important) touch points. As a result, Visionary Marketers generally go through the following five steps to map all of their touch points:

Step 1: Identify all touch points.

Step 2: Categorize the touch points that are part of the transaction, influence the transaction, and help to create the market context in which the transaction takes place (and therefore which matter most) and what role they play (or should play) in shaping customer behaviors.

Step 3: Identify the touch points they control versus those they influence.

Step 4: Map the touch points directly involved in closing the sale and the needs that their target customers have regarding these touch points; those that simply play an influential indirect role (for example, blogs showing customer reviews) versus touch points that play a contextual role (like Wall Street).

Step 5: Create a virtuous cycle of network building, managing, and influencing across all touch points.

By mapping out its network thoroughly, a company can holistically understand what might be required for stakeholders, at any particular touch point, to act in a manner aligned with the company's interests in closing the sale. An additional benefit of going through this network mapping exercise is that the results can be illuminating for the executive team. For the first time, many of them get a full appreciation of the many disparate groups that seem to care so much about the company and the brand.

Short- Versus Long-Term Touch Point Impact

Understanding the complex effects of a network can seem daunting for marketers, especially when they face top-line revenue and quarterly profitability targets among other pressures. Traditional or marketing communication marketers may feel mentally boxed in to do things the same way that they have always done them.

This is not surprising, given the results of a recent *State of Marketing Study* by Prophet of global CMOs in which many said they had limited influence over the major levers that drove business results but significant influence over traditional marketing communications levers. More important, these marketing leaders also believed that the traditional marketing vehicles—direct marketing, TV and print, point-of-sale merchandising—had the greatest short-term effectiveness. They did not believe that new communications tools had much utility in driving business results, and a significant number did not plan to pursue them. While marketers have always survived by sticking to well-understood tactics, our experience demonstrates that during the Network Era, such caution may lead to long-term brand erosion as the network evolves.

Conversely, these same marketers may overreact and feel compelled to make a dramatic shift into nontraditional marketing and networking venues, "as that is where it seems everyone is moving." The perceived urgency to move to Second Life and similar virtual worlds is an example of the overenthusiasm some have had in going digital, without any real plans on how best to leverage the medium in the future or show any return on investment. (Starwood's Aloft, an outstanding example of a plan to smartly leverage Second Life in the development of a new hotel brand, is discussed in the Third Shift.)

Visionary Marketers, however, look for the right balance of opportunities to build their business and brand for both the short and long term, assuming that building the right networked approach is simply part of their ongoing, integrated dialogue. At a minimum, marketers need to determine the impact that improved or aligned behavior at a key touch point might have in driving improved customer conversion. Mapping out your network, even if you don't act on it, will allow you to engage more thoughtfully in conversations in which your point of view has not been totally vetted.

For instance, in a recent client discussion about whether the client should spend $3 million on a thirty-second Super Bowl ad, the CMO had a hard time articulating what lift the company would receive by buying into the Super Bowl. His brand already had 100% awareness and very little new news. Of course, the ad would instill pride among employees (as well as investors and other stakeholders), but this CMO was almost sheepish in his defense of the pride effect. However, if he had fully mapped out his network, he would have seen how influential his employee base is in making the sale, both directly and indirectly, and how important this ad could be to bottom-line sales—albeit through building pride in his employees, not just communicating with his customers and prospects. To this point, when Bob Thacker, CMO of OfficeMax, was asked what his primary goals were in implementing the Elf Yourself viral video campaign, where viewers can upload photos and create elves of themselves or their friends or colleagues, or rolling out the world's biggest rubber-band ball, as certified by *Guinness World Records*, or his recent YouTube Penny Pranks, he said it was all tied to building corporate self-esteem, recognizing that his employee base was a critical influencing factor in how successful the business was. He also believed that the brand needed some personality and fun added to its staid persona. However, not in his wildest dreams did Thacker understand the power of the network effect in his simple pride-building ideas. When pressed about return on investment, Bob did have some numbers, as stated in a recent edition of *The Hub:*

> Well, with Elf Yourself, for example, the objective was really to brighten the brand, give it a face, make it charming and soften up people toward accepting the brand. We did measure how we did with it. We had 193 million or so people who Elf'ed themselves. Of those, 43 percent remembered OfficeMax. And of those, 37 percent said

it made them think more favorably about the company and more apt to shop there. So that, for what we wanted to do, was a good ROI because again, it was all about differentiation and internal pride building.

Living the Network Era's Success Principles: Apple

Apple is a good example of a company that has unlocked the value and power of its brand network. In fact, Apple has transformed its company by fully and successfully developing its brand network and targeting it in three basic respects.

First, Apple has a clear set of business objectives that forces management to continuously update its historic brand promise: to develop elegant products that integrate hardware and software in such a compelling fashion that consumer demand can reshape markets and consumer use can enable new behavior patterns. With every new product launch, techies, retailers, bloggers, journalists, and consumers anticipate what's next.

When Apple introduced the iPhone in 2007, the network effects were on overload, building on a similar approach deployed when the iPod was introduced. Now the stakes were even higher. Speculation had been rampant for months. Line drawings from patent filings had been debated as different camps attempted to divine what Apple might deliver. Apple tightly controlled what it could: the product specifications, the choice of network carrier, the execution of an elegant TV campaign. At the same time, it fueled the network through thoughtfully released comments, insider experiences for key bloggers, Steve Jobs's teasers, and so on. By the time of the product introduction, the active buying public already had such a detailed picture of the pros and cons of the device that it sold well even in the light of some well-publicized shortcomings. The network had essentially already internalized the negatives and determined that the product was worth buying.

Apple's second bead on developing networks is its clear understanding of the needs of key stakeholders: traditional hard-core loyalists, manufacturers of accessories and supporting products, channel partners, content partners, wireless carriers, the mainstream media, hundreds of technology and gadget blogs, and user groups. In addition, Apple builds its networks by aligning its commercial interests with those of its customers, partners, external influencers, and other companies. From exclusive music deals to Hollywood to Starbucks to Ford/GM/Mazda to the myriad of manufacturers of aftermarket accessories to Nike, each benefits if Apple succeeds and each helps to expand Apple's every increasing network (see Figure 2.3).

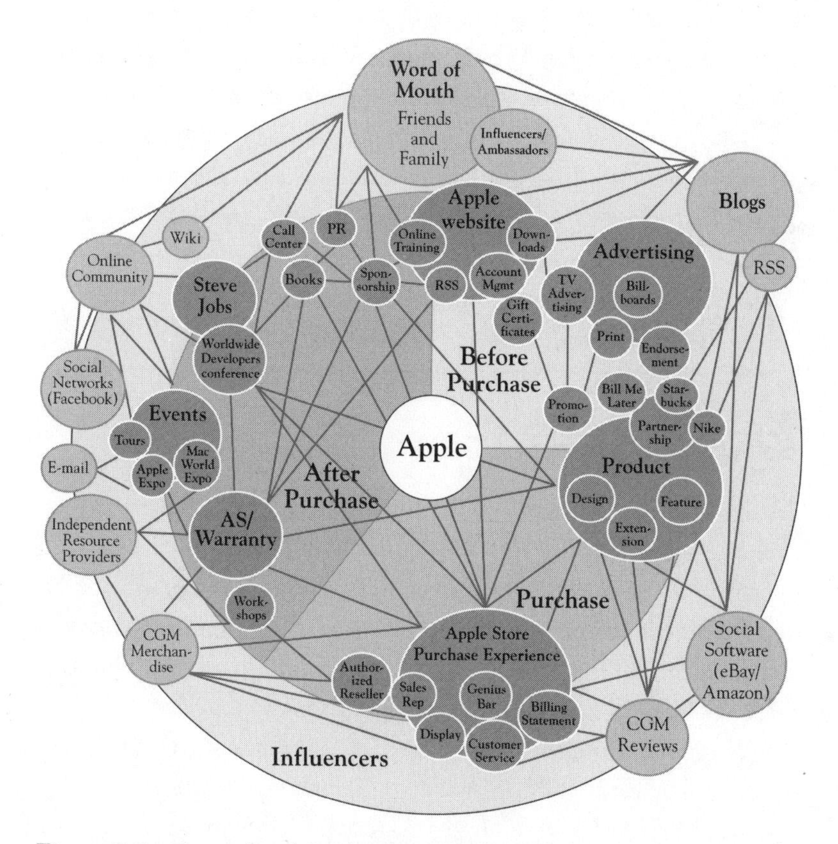

Figure 2.3 Example of Apple's Many Touch Points

To truly be authentic, Apple consistently listens to its network. Genius Bars (the tech support stations located in each Apple retail store) serve as Apple's commitment to superior customer service. In the Apple Stores, which have revolutionized the electronics retailer concept, superior customer service comes to life in the form of problem solving and troubleshooting and is helping build bigger loyalists out of Apple's customer base. People walk in with computer problems and walk out with their problems solved. In addition, the open layout with easy access to computers and iPods to experiment and play with while waiting for sales help make their wait bearable.

Why this approach works. Most marketers can find value in two repeating patterns of Apple's use of the brand network. First, although Apple used a product and offer strategy to extend its core brand promise, it still tightly controls the design and release of its offer. At the same time, it allows external stakeholders to find their personal and economic meaning in Apple's success. These network touch points are ruthless in their critique, inexhaustible in their interest, and dramatically important in ensuring Apple's success.

Apple's iPhone sold well over 10 million units within its first eighteen months, exceeding management's lofty goals.

So Why Isn't Everyone Galvanizing Their Network?

In any marketing program, vehicle, or tactic, a company must analyze the opportunities inherent in its brand network to see what aspects of it are most relevant to strategic success. While fully building and developing a social network may not be right for everyone, participating in the broader network is not optional. Your broader network is being built, whether you want it to be or not. Whether you choose to participate and drive that network, even in a modest way, is the question all Visionary Marketers must address.

Stephen Quinn of Walmart notes that the corporation has a market of 140 million customers every week. To deliver the right brand experience to them, enabling them to save money and live better lives, Marketing must always be looking at the right balance in investment between training, advertising, and merchandising versus developing a robust Network Era integration model. The reality is that it costs too much to do both well, and for Walmart, it is probably more important to get it right in the store and with the customer experience than to actively engage multiple stakeholders in the brand's network. However, ignoring the network is not an option either (see Walmart's very active blog). Every company must analyze the opportunities inherent in its brand network to see what aspects of it are most relevant to strategic success.

Mark Waller, Senior Vice President of Marketing and Sales for the National Football League (NFL), admits it has held back from exploiting all of the potential opportunities inherent in the sizable NFL Network. He admits that community and social media are perhaps the "'perfect tools' for the audience, but NFL.com is not community-based right now, it's not very interactive." Waller is held back by the sheer scale of his customer base:

> The size and scale of the audience we have is mind-blowing. How can we open up a community experience that reflects all of the NFL's values across an audience that big? This is very difficult. What content is allowable? How do we cater to the various groups? What mechanisms are needed to ensure it's truly representative of NFL values?

The NFL is like many other companies. Once the network is open for business, stakeholders they can only influence, rather than control, may have an even greater impact on sales than company-controlled communications. This is a scary proposition for companies.

Not every company is an Apple, Nike, or Adobe. However, it is valuable for everyone to take an exhaustive look at their network.

No matter what type of business you are in, large or small, you can bet that your customer base is finding ways to talk with one another.

As mentioned earlier, a new type of marketing, citizen marketing, has taken hold in the past few years. PQ Media's word-of-mouth marketing forecast indicates that overall spending on citizen marketing is expected to swell to almost $4 billion by 2011. These brand ambassador programs "hire" consumers, through incentives and rewards, to act as part PR agents, part sales reps, and part evangelists. They mix the spontaneity of buzz building with technology to instigate, guide, and measure what repeat customers are saying to each other about their brands. Even mainstream and traditional marketers have taken this route.

Unilever's 2007–08 "Go Green and Small with All," which used in-classroom magazine and web ads to recruit participants, targeting elementary school children through a contest looking for the greenest elementary school in the country. Its ambassadors were encouraged to get their families to make small green changes at home (like using concentrated All detergent) and to spread branded, eco-friendly messages. The ambassadors and their parents submitted report cards on their progress, and the school with the highest percentage of report cards received a $50,000 grant for eco-friendly school improvements, a solar-powered iPod Shuffle MP3 player for every student, a one-year supply of All, and an appearance on *The Ellen DeGeneres Show*. More than three thousand elementary schools entered.

JetBlue's BlueDay, now in its third year, is one of the more established college-style ambassador events. Held in the fall on twenty-one campuses on the East Coast and in northern California, students wear blue costumes (and, on occasion, color their skin and hair blue), and those with the best costumes are given a pair of free airline tickets.

Why do these models work? In a world of finite marketing investment funds and exploding numbers of interested stakeholders, it is impossible to spend enough to control a network. The only available strategy for many companies is to find a way to make it beneficial for stakeholders to behave in a way that furthers a company's strategy.

To this point, a new type of brand advocate has risen up recently, and it's not the technophiles blogging to each other about new widgets and gadgets. It's the "gamma women": those who influence a wide network of consumers and generate and disseminate new ideas and trends. The number of gamma women in America is estimated at 55 million and growing, according to "Gamma Women," a report from Meredith Corporation.

Gammas may be as well off financially as alpha males, but their choices express their creativity and personal style, making their homes comfortable and welcoming, and doing their part to preserve the environment, according to Meredith. "Gammas are true brand advocates who are passionate and spread the word about what they like," said Jack Griffin, President of Meredith Publishing. "It's time for marketers to engage Gammas where they are already looking for social currency—talking with them versus talking at them."

So, What Do I Do on Monday Morning?

Here are a few things to consider in your organization as you think about shifting your organization from controlling the message to galvanizing your network:

1. Clearly understand the benefits associated with establishing or building a networked approach for your company. Understand how this aligns with your company's growth objectives and imperatives.
2. Have a clear understanding of why fully leveraging and managing a networked approach, at its broadest level, has or has not taken hold in your organization and what the missing ingredient is for your organization to fully embrace and then accept a networked approach.

3. Use customer research and insights to fully understand how customers want to participate and interact with your brand going forward. What are their needs, wants, and relationship expectations from your company?
4. Map your company's world of touch points, using Apple's touch point map as a guide, to provide an exhaustive picture of all of the touch points directly or indirectly influencing the purchase decision.
5. From your exhaustive list of touch points, determine which are directly involved in value delivery, which influence the purchase decision, and which shape the market context in which your organization operates.
6. Develop a plan of action in regard to these touch points that are directly involved in the value delivery or influence the purchase decision, recognizing that the return on investment on those shaping the market context will not be high.
7. Start making small investments in a few networks to show the impact they have on purchase consideration and decisions, with a particular focus on touch points that have an influencing effect on the purchase decision (such as FlyerTalk).
8. Determine your digital point of view. Operating in a networked world is not all about going digital, but the landscape has changed enough so that an absence of participation is almost as noticeable as is overparticipation.
9. Map out your company's future state touch point map, highlighting the areas you see investing in or making bets on in the future. Develop measures that will help you understand how well you are or are not doing as you start to build out your network.
10. Get going. Start small, and recognize that you are on a networked journey. Pick a part of the organization in which you want to build out a network. You'll be surprised how

early network wins can begin to change the internal dialogue around control versus influence.

Now that you have seen how Visionary Marketers can help their organizations move to an influence model by tapping into all of the touch points across their network, it is important to see next how Visionary Marketers can fully leverage that network, as well as other organizational assets, from an innovation perspective. In this way, they can help transform their organization into having a truly pervasive innovation mind-set in the Third Shift: from incremental improvements to pervasive innovation.

3

THE THIRD SHIFT

From Incremental Improvements to Pervasive Innovation

It is hard to define where innovation begins and ends for us. In order to do better, year over year, you need to constantly innovate and try and reinvent yourself. I can no longer distinguish between which parts of my job are innovation-oriented and which are not."

Barry Judge, CMO of Best Buy, has obviously internalized this Third Shift, which we define as moving from incremental improvements to pervasive innovation—innovation that can come from anywhere and can have an impact everywhere. Innovation is pervasive in everything Judge and his Best Buy counterparts think and do in order to profitably grow. From Geek Squad (tech support) to Magnolia (in-home theater) to Rewards Zones (loyalty program) to its recently launched musical instrument store within a store, Best Buy continues to see innovation as its lifeblood and looks to Marketing to help lead the charge.

Ann Lewnes, Senior Vice President of Corporate Marketing for Adobe, has also taken this perspective, and as a result, marketing at Adobe has shifted to playing a much greater role in the company's innovation efforts and thus the overall growth agenda.

For the most recent launch of its creative flagship software, Adobe Creative Suite 4, the combined efforts of the business unit and marketing teams ensured that not only were the products truly market-ready but the launch was market inclusive, providing multiple ways for the myriad of users to be involved.

To ensure market readiness, selected product betas were posted to a website, inviting a selection of users to play with and provide feedback on the product as it was being developed. The website, called Adobe Labs, is aimed at fostering a collaborative, interactive process where users can shape new products according to the users' (not the company's) needs and preferences.

To ensure market inclusiveness, the team developed a multipronged approach that used all touch points with customers, from traditional media to social networks, to reach the broadest global audience. It included a "rolling New Year's Eve" web event, which allowed users globally to register for their local launch—essentially a webcast streamed to their region at an allotted time. Content and creative was available in more than twenty-nine languages on Adobe.com, reaching more than a hundred markets. And through a truly innovative medium, called Adobe TV, education and training were provided with over a hundred new feature demos and over two hundred video workshop tutorials presented by Product Managers and Evangelists.

Adobe has worked hard internally to fuse the company's world-class engineering and software design, with cutting-edge approaches to solicit ongoing customer feedback to drive innovations that are market tested and ready for sale. The benefits to Adobe's overall approach to open innovation are many: superior end products, built-in market advocacy, preexisting sales before the actual launch, and, ultimately, increased customer loyalty. The drawback to this co-creation and open innovation approach is, as Lewnes readily admits, the need to be "comfortable with a certain loss of control," a consistent theme throughout *The Shift*. This is a trade-off Adobe has felt comfortable making. As Lewnes notes, "It is a powerful way to make people feel that they are a part of the brand."

Exciting things are happening in how organizations innovate—exciting especially because innovation has always been so hard, for reasons you may already understand and that are discussed later in this chapter. But marketers and organizations have new mind-sets and resources that are making it easier to master this art and help to make innovation pervasive throughout the organization.

Visionary Marketers should consider the diverse yet expansive set of examples we discuss in this chapter as they develop and lead a new approach to innovation for their organization—one that goes beyond the norm and allows innovation to occur everywhere and come from anywhere. This is why we call it pervasive innovation. It is now Visionary Marketers' moment in time to take a leadership role in helping to infuse this into the DNA of their organizations.

Pervasive Innovation

Pervasive innovation is not a particularly new idea; however, it is often not well understood. Traditional incremental innovation is usually defined by new products, new services, new offerings, and the successful management of a new product pipeline. Most innovation efforts occur at a business unit, divisional, or functional level, and thus most innovation efforts are insular and siloed, and not always harnessing the myriad inputs at the company's disposal. Also, most innovations are traditionally aimed at driving top-line revenues, not margin (although it is generally implied). This is traditional textbook innovation or new product development, defined in a vertical, mostly nonholistic way, usually resulting in incremental improvements. Traditional innovation definitely serves a purpose,

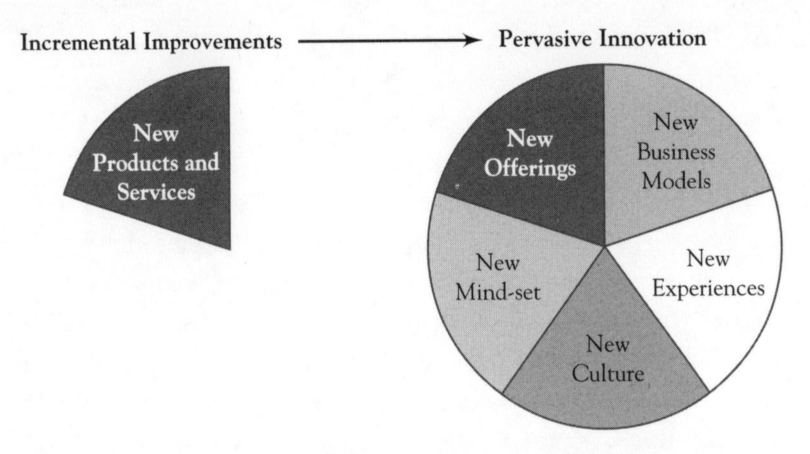

Figure 3.1 Incremental Improvements Versus Pervasive Innovation

but there is an opportunity to ratchet the concept up a notch to what we are calling pervasive innovation.

Pervasive innovation doesn't live within a function, it is not an annual exercise, and it does not necessarily have to fill the growth gap on its own. Instead, pervasive innovation is a mind-set incorporating all fresh and new ideas, aimed at improving a business's overall performance, inside and outside the organization. Pervasive innovation of course includes new products, new services, and new offerings, but it can also include new business models, new experiences, new cultures, new mind-sets—basically new ideas—to solve old and new problems inside and outside the company (Figure 3.1). Pervasive innovation is a way of life, part of a company's DNA, and the lifeline for many companies to meet all of their future aspirations. Think of Dell, GE, Google, P&G, Toyota, and Apple, and you are thinking correctly about pervasive innovation.

A Shift Toward Customer-Led Innovation

As companies recognize this need for pervasive innovation, Visionary Marketers like Lewnes can use their knowledge base of customer insights to demonstrate how they can have an impact on all drivers of the company's growth agenda. In particular, and as a key entry point in demonstrating how Marketing can help create growth, some of the best marketing leaders have pushed for a new customer-led innovation mind-set in service of helping to maximize a company's chances for new product success.

This is important because, although figures vary, the result is still the same: CEOs aren't happy with the current method of innovating and with the commensurate results. According to a 2008 Boston Consulting Group survey on measuring innovation, two-thirds of companies consider innovation one of their top three strategic priorities; however, 57% are not satisfied with their return on innovation efforts. Thus, Visionary Marketers need to be prepared to argue and prove that because marketers can connect customer insights with a solid business acumen, as discussed in the First Shift, they can help lead innovation efforts to drive higher levels of innovation success, and therefore executive satisfaction. This ability will help the leadership team gain greater confidence in its overall innovation program and help to revolutionize their company's innovation productivity, all with an eye on profitable growth. Visionary Marketers ultimately need to see innovation as both a means and an end to achieving short- and long-term company success.

In addition to Adobe and Best Buy, other companies have revolutionized their mind-set and approach to innovation over the past several years, creating impressive track records of innovation success—and profitable growth. Procter & Gamble, Google, GE, and Cargill have all changed their innovation mind-sets and approaches to effectively *innovate* how they go about innovation. In each case, one of the hallmarks is a shift to involving multiple stakeholders in shaping their innovation output:

- *Procter & Gamble expands beyond its R&D lab as a source of innovation.* P&G CEO A. G. Lafley states that innovation is "purpose driven, people led and the heart of our business model." In 2003, when he realized the company's age-old R&D-centric innovation model could no longer achieve the levels of growth he, his board, and shareholders demanded, he ordered P&G to move from a strictly R&D-driven system to an open innovation system. P&G now takes its customer insight knowledge generated by the marketing teams and translates the top consumer needs into science-based problems. It then creates technology briefs defining the problems and articulating the desired requirements for success. P&G then reaches out to a worldwide network of technology entrepreneurs who seek to solve these consumer needs. Internally termed Connect and Develop (C&D), this system infinitely expands the scope of ideas by enabling P&G to tap into experts worldwide. C&D has already resulted in more than a thousand active innovations that are either partially or entirely driven by external development. More important, it has helped launch hundreds of new products, including household favorites Olay Regenerist, Swiffer products, and the Crest SpinBrush.

- *Google embraces ongoing innovation as a way of life.* Google's phenomenal success is based on its approach to innovation. Google is innovation. The company's well-publicized nine-point innovation strategy ranges from "Innovation, not instant perfection," to "Get users and usage—the money will follow." In Google language, getting users and usage is equivalent to the tried-and-true notions of customer feedback and insight, again all coming back to how well those leading the innovation charge understand their customers' needs, wants, and desires. Since everyone in the company realizes it will succeed or fail based on ongoing innovation, it's not surprising when great results happen. A key to Google's ongoing innovation success is employee participation. Employees are provided time and incentives to innovate, resulting in a true culture of innovation, as well as a track record of having multiple employee-generated, in-market Google innovation successes.

- *Cargill's brand stands for Collaborate, Create, Succeed.* Cargill's mission is to be the global leader in nourishing people, and its innovation efforts stem from both its customers and employees. Cargill motivates its employees to listen to customer needs, understand the insights drawn from these interactions and uses the company's resources to solve those needs. According to Ann Ness, Vice President of Corporate Brand Management, "Innovation awards, which are coveted and celebrated, motivate employees to be part of a team that connects with other business unit teams to come up with innovation efforts that will help enhance customer relationships." Ness also observes, "It has become easy to trace many of these awards back to a distinct market need that one of our employees heard about from a customer." Ness has made sure that Marketing's voice is strong in all innovation efforts and that helping to orchestrate and drive a voice of the customer mind-set—listening to customers 24/7—has been one of the most important assets Marketing has helped add to Cargill's growth agenda.
- *GE's imagination is always at work, as it continues to break through with big ideas.* Jeff Immelt established the $100 million breakthrough concept a few years back to help energize organic sales and better harness the power of the different lines of business, which at times got too mired in the day-to-day business to "imagine what if?" Immelt created a system to push innovation throughout the organization. He required business unit teams to submit

at least three Imagination Breakthrough (IB) proposals each year that would ultimately go before GE's version of an innovation and growth council for review and discussion. The projects, which ultimately would receive billions of dollars in investment funding and be expected to generate tens of billions of dollars of new sales, have to meet two criteria to be considered investment-worthy: each idea needs to take GE into a new line of business, geographical area, or customer base; and if the idea does not have $100 million potential within its first few years, don't bother. Through 2007, IBs accounted for $30 billion in new revenues based on $7 billion in investments—not a bad return on investment!

Before these mind-sets took hold, all of these companies knew that they were not fully realizing their innovation potential and not harnessing the opportunity to leverage multiple internal and external stakeholders and resources to maximize their innovation efforts in a truly pervasive way. Importantly, the companies highlighted above dared their employees to take risks in innovating and to use multiple sources of inspiration to innovate and try to break through to big ideas, for internal or external application, significantly multiplying their chances for success. Each of these companies has stressed that innovation can come from anywhere and impact everywhere. And each of these companies has recognized that Marketing has had to, and will continue to, play a significant role in driving this new mind-set forward.

Visionary Marketers' Innovative Moment in Time

You might be thinking, "Wow, pervasive innovation sounds exciting, and I clearly see a driving role for Marketing. Sign me up!"

Not so fast. The reality is that despite the need for more leadership, activity, and results, Marketing historically has rarely played a driving role in a company's innovation efforts. Understandably, R&D, Engineering, Merchandising, business unit heads, or other organizational leaders may view themselves as the leaders in innovation within their respective organizations and Marketing an enabler, at best. In fact, in the previously referenced Boston Consulting Group's innovation study, only 5% of respondents said that Marketing is the driving force in innovation today.

Nevertheless, many of the marketers interviewed for this book believe there may be no single area within their organization more equipped and more underleveraged in helping to drive innovation efforts forward than Marketing, especially as this pervasive world of innovation begins to emerge. Thus, Visionary Marketers may have a unique moment in time to take on a more substantive innovation leadership role as many of the demands brought on by *The Shift,* as evidenced by Google, P&G, GE, and others, require the same skill set, knowledge base, and leveraging of external networks that a Visionary Marketer commands. Walmart's Stephen Quinn sums it up: "Marketing could and should provide tremendous value to innovation." If you agree with Quinn, then most likely you agree that Visionary Marketers and Marketing overall has to become a core innovation enabler.

What this requires of Visionary Marketers are the previously discussed skills and mind-sets: deep expertise, leading by example, great ability to collaborate, P&L mind-set, willingness to take risks, customer advocacy, and so forth—all attributes described throughout *The Shift.* To make innovation pervasive, Visionary Marketers also need an integrated view of art and science; depth in customer intimacy, industry, and broader macrotrends; and a constant eye on what competitors are and are not doing. Marketers must also own and leverage the network connections that round out a pervasive innovation mind-set—customer communities, roster agencies, multiple distributors, and supplier relationships in place—to truly take advantage of the incredible asset bases the organization has access to.

As stated, Marketing can never own pervasive innovation (no one function can), but Visionary Marketers can play a significant role in bringing a pervasive innovation mind-set to life. And importantly, as discussed in the First Shift, Marketing has the ability to help articulate and drive the growth agenda and ultimately align a company's innovation and growth strategy, an important first step in establishing the right role for marketers in innovation, going forward.

Why Innovation Efforts Fall Short: A Visionary Marketers' Opportunity

There are multiple reasons that innovation efforts continue to underperform relative to initial expectations. Some of the more important ones include:

- Lack of a well-articulated innovation strategy
- Lack of a well-developed innovation culture
- Lack of confidence in innovation efforts tied to lack of previous success
- Lack of a top-down mandate and CEO-led focus
- Lack of overall skill sets, capabilities, and competencies
- Lack of ability to generate new ideas
- Lack of cross-company collaboration, coordination, and integration (R&D versus Marketing)

While all of these failure factors are important to acknowledge, the one that probably gets the least attention, and may have the greatest impact of all, is lack of confidence. In fact, according to a recent McKinsey Quarterly, *How Companies Approach Innovation*, 60% of corporate leaders say they are not confident in their own ability to execute on innovation. John Nottingham, cofounder of the innovation consultancy Nottingham-Spirk, tries to explain that this lack of confidence might be tied to all of the innovation unknowns out there today: "Five to ten years ago it was all about reengineering, efficiency gains, and global sourcing to get your act together. Now, what's next? What's new? How do we innovate to add value? Where are the big ideas and the small ones to nourish the big ones? What are the risks we are willing to take?"

Summing up the major innovation issues and impediments, there appear to be three primary reasons that innovation efforts fall short (especially in the CEO's eyes), representing a tremendous opportunity for Visionary Marketers to step up and change the innovation dialogue going forward:

- *The organization is plagued by lack of an innovation strategy and a short-term myopia.* "We need to make our strategy more relevant." "We aren't growing as fast as we used to." "Customers no longer find our products, services, or brand relevant." "Our margins are decreasing, and we're losing market share." "We know we need to reinvent our company, but we don't know how." "We need to identify new markets, growth segments, and white space opportunities." "We talk long term, but everything is really about the next two quarters."
- *No one in the company knows where to begin, and no one seems to have the competencies to get there.* "We're not Google. Our people don't feel passionate about innovation." "Even our best and brightest won't engage to innovate." "Our culture is too risk averse to encourage innovation." "Leadership talks innovation but doesn't give the resources to support it." "We lack the capabilities (and guts) to truly innovate."
- *The company has real difficulty in generating good ideas.* "We need new and improved offerings for growth, but

> our pipeline is dry." "We don't have enough insights to drive breakthrough ideas." "We don't have enough fresh perspectives about customers and the market." "We lack the tools, the processes, and the best practices of other organizations to help us understand how to best attack the fuzzy front end."

There is truly a lot of work to be done to move the pervasive innovation needle. And this is the opportunity for a Visionary Marketer to lead a new dialogue around innovation and help their company see the possibilities, as opposed to the limitations. Someone needs to step up and help recast the entire notion to one of pervasive innovation. Short of the CEO taking this on exclusively, as with the other shifts, why shouldn't the Visionary Marketer be the one to start leading this dialogue?

Where Visionary Marketers Can Shine

It behooves Visionary Marketers to take a fresh look at the role Marketing could play in helping to transform internal innovation efforts in service of eventually helping their company bring a pervasive innovation mind-set to life. For instance, Visionary Marketers can start to play a larger role in innovation by consistently demonstrating how customer insights can make a difference to the success of their company's innovation efforts. It is the marketers' keen understanding of customer insights—the experiences, delights, frustrations, and unmet needs that influence customer behavior—that can inform the innovation process on one level and broader strategic growth on another. This ultimately leads Marketing to play a greater driver role with more innovation accountability.

To this point, Beth Comstock, CMO for GE, recalls that early on, "We said that Marketing should share in innovation. That was very confusing at first because Marketing was considered a communications function. However, Jeff Immelt knew that GE should expect more from Marketing and thus said that we should have top-line responsibilities for growth. In the early days, it was defining the basics of marketing, but we are now evolving into a strategy and an understanding of what it takes to innovate."

With Immelt's encouragement, Comstock has developed marketing-led approaches for business units and Corporate Marketing to capture and leverage a deeper understanding of customers and customer insights. She shares these approaches with innovation teams throughout GE and has seen innovation efforts throughout continue to improve.

Similarly, Brian Swette, formerly of Burger King, states, "The Marketing group has started to grow new concepts using all of the sources of ideas and insights it has at its hands. As an example, one of the things that we wanted to drive was new access points in more exciting, deliberate ways." The result, through numerous inputs, was the launch of the Whopper Bar, a smaller format restaurant that sells up to ten types of the famous burger, where customers have the choice to create their own Whopper with a variety of toppings. Burger King's Whopper Bar was inspired by Marketing. Marketing understood that its core customer was a male who worked in construction and would not respond favorably to the trend toward healthy eating. The Whopper Bar squarely addresses the needs of its core consumers while celebrating Burger King's signature item, the Whopper. "In most companies, Marketing would be the last place where a new store design would emerge," says Swette. He also quickly acknowledges that without all of the other core functions required to bring the Whopper Bar to life from the day the idea surfaced, it would not have been nearly as successful as it is. Swette and the Burger King team clearly go to market with a pervasive innovation mind-set.

In addition, industry and trend data can pave the way for a deeper understanding of customer behavior, current and future, and are powerful sources of inspiration. Although it is not as powerful as one-on-one interactions, Visionary Marketers' ability to integrate different data sources can provide a decent substitute. Here again, access to this data and a deep understanding of how to interpret the data should fall squarely in the marketer's domain, as should leading the dialogue on engaging with customers in their environment.

The Payoff of Sustainable, Pervasive Innovation

A world-class pervasive innovation mind-set and approach can drive incredible companywide benefits:

- *Greater relevancy*. Relevancy is about being important, pertinent, and useful for customers. Whether it is new products, services, channels of distribution, or customer experiences, consistently meeting and exceeding customers' unique needs will continue to make and keep your brand relevant.
- *Improved differentiation*. A company's products, services, and experiences must be innovative to stand out against those of the competition, putting real distance between the company and its strongest competitor.
- *Increased brand value*. Brands represent one of the company's most tangible and highly valuable assets. When relevancy and differentiation are achieved, increased brand value will follow. Innovation helps brands and businesses thrive, regardless of external circumstances or other challenges.
- *Financial returns*. At the end of the day, it's all about the bottom line. In order to be prioritized, any business initiative needs to make sense, and innovation is no exception. When innovation efforts are pursued appropriately, they have the potential to drive positive financial results more than any other type of initiative.
- *Energized employees*. This innovation benefit is often overlooked. Whether at corporate headquarters or in

the field, everyone likes to be involved in innovation in some way. Companies that successfully embrace innovation tend to have employees who are both motivated and high performing.

- *Market leadership*. Another big benefit of a sustainable and pervasive innovation mind-set and approach is enjoying a leading market position that will yield price premiums, analyst favoritism, and a cushion during trying economic times.

As evidence, leading innovators continuously look to build cultures that think about innovation and its contributors in good and bad times. "Strong companies understand this, and during a recession, they invest," says Eric Schmidt, chairman and CEO of Google, and they often get pummeled for it: 'How could you do this? You're arrogant. The world is falling apart.' Figure 3.2 shows how Google benefits from pervasive innovation.

Recent studies support these points. *Profit Impact of Market Strategy*, a British study of a thousand businesses during the past

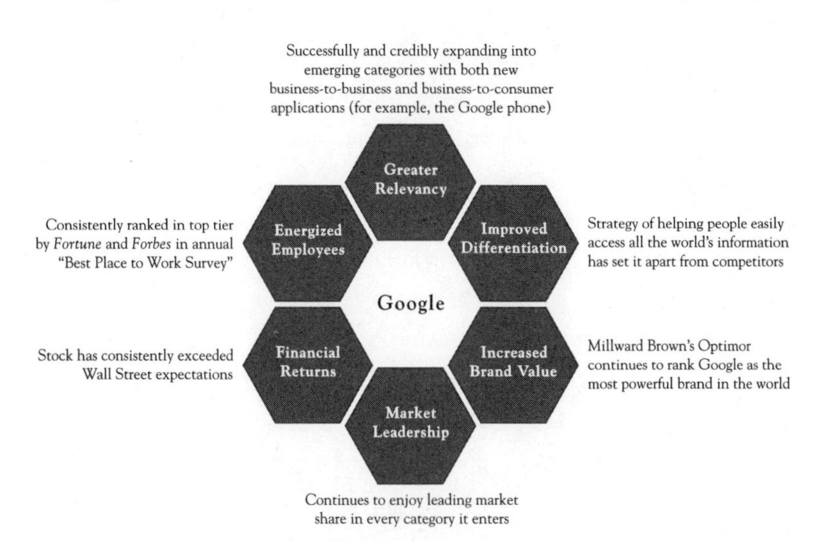

Figure 3.2 How Google Benefits from Pervasive Innovation

thirty years, for example, found that companies that spent more on innovation during a downturn saw return on capital employed rise 23.8% during the recovery compared with 0.6% for those that slashed spending. Smart companies, companies that practice pervasive innovation, and their Visionary Marketers have learned that it is better to prepare to grow during a downturn than to just slash spending and be completely unprepared when the market turns up.

What Visionary Marketers Can Learn from Model Innovators

Model Innovators is our term for the profile, characteristics, and dynamics that comprise leading, innovative companies. In making a case for a new and refreshed perspective on innovation, Andy Stefanovich of Play, a Prophet company, says, "Pervasive Innovation has to become a philosophy. The most innovative companies do not demand that their innovation process only produce new products and services; instead, like Google, they foster a philosophy of innovation that pervades the company and its networks, and it usually starts from the top."

Recently Prophet conducted a study with Play, surveying over 150 senior strategists, innovators, and marketers about their innovation practices. Within this research, some patterns started to emerge that point to the Model Innovator concept. The study sought to uncover what successful innovation companies are doing right, how to create winning formulas, how to overcome barriers to innovation, and where Marketing best fits. It was clear that there was a break between the haves and have-nots: between those who understand pervasive innovation and those who still see new product development as the end game; between those who consistently saw better-than-average returns on their investment dollars and those who did not. The companies that got it, the Model Innovators, generally were those that lived by these guiding principles, developing and working within a balanced ecosystem:

- Leadership catalysts: Company leaders are the catalysts for growth through a well-defined pervasive innovation strategy supported and driven by the leadership team, including (and perhaps especially) marketers.
- Expansive network of partners, customers, suppliers, distributors, industry thought leaders, and even competitors must be tapped into seamlessly and continuously drive pervasive innovation efforts forward.
- Competencies and cultural dynamics supportive of a pervasive innovation mind-set.

Leadership Catalysts, Starring Visionary Marketers

Visionary Marketers within Model Innovator companies embrace innovation as a critical growth engine and see it in a pervasive way. They help define, communicate, and implement an ongoing innovation strategy that is aligned with the overall corporate strategy. Their employees not only understand the role of innovation within the broader business strategy, but also articulate that role clearly to others. Model innovator leaders engage others across the organization, realizing that success is no longer limited to an individual, a function, or a division. Says Mark Waller of the NFL, "As an executive team, we own innovation. Marketing owns grounding it in what the consumers/fans want and creating the process to engage the broader organization and the executive team into driving successful in-market execution."

As CEO of IBM, Sam J. Palmisano announced a few years back in a *BusinessWeek* article by J. McGregor, "The only way you will thrive in this business environment is by constantly innovating—innovating in technologies, innovating in strategies, innovating in business models." Palmisano made it clear from the start that no one on the executive team was excused from innovation and that pervasive innovation was going to be a way of life for IBM. When

Palmisano made this declaration, it was obvious that IBM was no longer going to be the big-box, product-dominated organization it had been for decades, and that the entire executive team was going to need to embrace a new beginning for the organization. This would be one in which not just R&D and engineering drove innovation; every function would have to become part of the solution to this challenge to thrive.

Obviously pervasive innovation requires strong leadership and a clear and consistent strategy from the top. Some of the most prolific innovators and leaders of all time—Steve Jobs, Howard Schultz, Richard Branson, Charles Schwab—are all Archetype I leaders and organizations. They stand out because of their bold visions for the future, their ability to clearly articulate strategies to deliver on that vision and their willingness to take risks to execute those strategies. Even so, you don't need a Steve Jobs or Michael Dell to drive innovation throughout your organization. As Russ Klein, Ann Lewnes, and Becky Saeger can all attest to, Marketing can play a significant leadership role in helping to shape and articulate the innovation agenda.

An inherent final part of a Visionary Marketer's role and responsibility for catalyzing an organization around pervasive innovation is the constant pushing of the organization to keep asking, "What business are we really in?" Helping your organization know and expand its frame of reference can provide it with a much wider canvas on which to innovate. Barry Judge of Best Buy, for example, believes his insightful reworking of the company's frame of reference helped it dramatically expand the way it thought about its customers. He says, "Marketing helped the company to realize that we were not in technology or electronics sales [functionally based], as we had always emphasized, but rather that we were in the business of fulfilling customers' wildest dreams." The former assumption is a limiting, feature-based frame of reference that leads to extinction, while the latter provides a long-term path to growth.

Similarly, when Adam Stotsky, President of NBC Marketing and former head of Marketing for the Sci-Fi Network, guided his organization to expand its frame of reference beyond providing high-quality, genre-based programming (functionally based) to that of providing its audience with transformative escapes, its aperture for new ideas—and growth—widened dramatically. By adopting a wider brand and business lens based on an expansive view of customers and the benefits they seek, and not simply offerings, companies can continue to reinvent themselves while staying true to their strengths. A broader frame of reference can lead to new experiences, additional sources of revenue, and altogether transformed categories.

The Merging of the Second and Third Shifts: An Expansive Network Leads to an Expansive Mind-Set

At this point, it is important to bring together the powers and interdependencies within the Second and Third Shifts—the role an expanded network can play in helping companies truly realize a pervasive approach to innovation, fully accessing all of the assets and inputs it has at its disposal.

Visionary Marketers can become the hub inside the network wheel, connecting all of the internal and external networks and data sources together to look for the newest, biggest, and best ideas. They can help to look beyond the traditional walls for sources of inspiration from anyone: employees, customers, competitors, vendors and suppliers, consultants, universities, and online communities including bloggers. Visionary Marketers can use this network before, during, and after innovation efforts as well as throughout the course of trying to build a lasting, loyalty-based relationship with customers.

The Power of Open Innovations and Environments

Henry Chesbrough, a professor at the University of California Berkeley's Haas Business School, where he teaches and runs the Center for Open Innovation, argues that the old closed (functional) innovation model—vertically integrated research-and-development departments that develop technology in-house for the sole use of their corporate parent—is becoming obsolete in an age of mobile scientific workers, ubiquitous high-tech start-ups, and a growing extra-corporate research establishment at university labs. To partake more fully in the benefits of an open innovation model, Chesbrough believes companies need to develop the ability to experiment with their business models, find ways to open them up, and ultimately do very little of their own basic research. They need to drop the do-it-all-yourself approach and pioneer methods of importing ideas from everywhere and letting their own innovations enter the wider marketplace to develop and evolve.

Model Innovator companies are open to sourcing and improving ideas outside their R&D departments and outside the company. Seeing their penchant for connecting for success, other companies are following suit by expanding networks to employees, customers, partners, and resourceful entrepreneurs.

Two examples of where open innovation thrives are the company Nottingham-Spirk and the philosophy behind P&G's Connect and Develop model.

Nottingham-Spirk In her article for *Fortune*, "Ideas Made Here," Anne Fisher referred to Nottingham-Spirk as "the most successful industrial design firm you've probably never heard of." The Ohio-based product innovation and development firm currently holds 517 commercialized patents, and the combined sales of products created by Nottingham-Spirk exceed $30 billion. Company founders John Nottingham and John Spirk helped to pioneer open innovation; they get ideas from anywhere and collaborate with stakeholders across the board to ensure their new products win in the market. "The key to success is that 'open' means 'open.' Don't close down ideas and don't set constraints," advises Nottingham, "because when multiple parties are working together towards a common goal, decisions and actions tend to happen faster." Many innovation firms tout an end-to-end approach to innovation, but Nottingham-Spirk truly embodies it. The company leads clients on a journey from initial customer insights all the way through to market-ready product and service launches. It leverages multiple sources of inspiration—researchers, designers, engineers, customers, and suppliers—all helping to collaboratively and ultimately compress the time it takes to go from a piece of paper to on the shelf.

P&G's Connect and Develop (C&D) As mentioned, P&G's open innovation system, Connect and Develop (C&D), is designed to identify and acquire existing innovations that satisfy P&G business needs. Although most of the acquisitions through C&D are intended to expand core areas, Procter & Gamble continuously seeks innovation initiatives directed at new businesses, channels, or consumers. By collaborating externally around the world, P&G systematically searches for technologies, packages, and products with proven consumer interest or success. With C&D, P&G now taps into creativity and talent from over 1.5 million people around the world, a far cry more than its admittedly impressive internal research network of seventy-five hundred.

The Power of Customer Co-Creation

Co-creation can be defined as an open, ongoing collaboration between employees and customers to define and create products, services, experiences, ideas, and information, all in the service of pushing whatever is in development forward. It aims to foster a collaborative, interactive process where users can shape new products according to their (not the company's) needs and preferences, in advance of a formal product launch, so that ultimately the innovation is market tested and ready for sale. The benefits, as mentioned in the Adobe example earlier, include superior end products, built-in market advocacy, preexisting sales before the actual launch, and, ultimately, increased customer loyalty.

"Open" implies transparency; nonparticipants can easily see the collaborative process. "Ongoing" implies more than a one-time shot at obtaining customer input and then taking the rest of it in-house. Anyone can participate, at any time. "Collaboration" brings in the spirit of teamwork. Employees and customers are peers in the process. In many cases, the company simply serves as a facilitator of the process. Tangible examples of successful customer co-creations include Boeing's 787 Dreamliner and Starwood's Aloft hotel.

Boeing 787 Dreamliner Although the economic environment and a few production delays have slowed the launch of Boeing's 787 Dreamliner, the Dreamliner story nonetheless provides a great example of the power of customer co-creation.

According to a *BtoB Magazine* article in October 2006, Rob Pollack, Vice President of Brand and Market Positioning, Boeing Commercial Aircraft, was the first to admit to the risks in getting creative "when the product you're trying to create and market costs more than $5 billion to develop." But taking a few risks is exactly what Boeing needed to do, according to Pollack, who joined the company's commercial airplane segment in 2002 to lead a new strategic marketing team. Pollack opted to rejuvenate the company from the inside out, starting with a new brand promise, "revolutionizing flight," to encourage employees to think boldly. It also decided to jump-start interest in the development of its first new passenger aircraft since the 777 was introduced in 1990. Under Pollack's guidance, early on, Boeing forged a marketing alliance with AOL Time Warner to allow AOL members and nonmembers alike to go online to vote for one of four possible names for the plane. Dreamliner was the winning name.

At the same time, Boeing created a world-class design team of aircraft enthusiasts and industry insiders who were consulted throughout the design and development process. Boeing took co-creation even further by bringing partners and suppliers, in addition to customers, into the process. Boeing has created a fully collaborative work environment up and down the value chain. How does Boeing engage customers in the innovation process? For starters, it launched the Passenger Experience Research Center (PERC), a facility next to the Boeing Tour Center in Everett, Washington, which allows the company to solicit input on the airplane's design from visitors from around the world. In order to do this, PERC features a scale model of the 787 Dreamliner aircraft's interior cabin design and welcomes the public to "test-drive" and provide opinions on the cabin's comfort and aesthetics as well as their preference on everything from cabin width to overhead stowage space. This immediate and direct feedback enables the Dreamliner team to test full-scale designs and rapidly iterate new ideas critical to the airplane's design. Importantly, this feedback loop has helped Boeing energize the public about the Dreamliner and reach its overall objective of "rejuvenating the spirit of travel."

"We have been thinking about the Dreamliner in stages," Pollack said. "Remotivating an organization that had become a little too arrogant—that was the first stage. The second stage was talking to the industry about the changes we were making. The final part will be convincing the flying public that they will prefer flying on a Boeing airplane." By adopting a pervasive innovation mind-set and co-creating the Dreamliner with customers and employees around the world, Boeing may indeed get customers to start to align with the manufacturer instead of the airline. We believe the Dreamliner is poised to take off and be a tremendous success, fundamentally changing the dynamics of the airline industry.

Starwood Aloft In 2007, Starwood Hotels became the first company in history to open a new hotel brand inside a virtual world. Starwood Hotels redefined the concept of co-creation with its virtual hotel, which invited customers to experience the hotel from the comfort of their computers and, in the process, interact with the designers and architects who build the actual hotel. The virtual hotel gives guests the ability to check into a room, relax in the lobby, exercise in the fitness center, and partake in virtually any other activity associated with a typical hotel stay. The benefits associated with this type of customer co-creation are numerous. First, Starwood ensured that the eventual design of the brick-and-mortar version of the hotel would meet the exacting standards of its most loyal and important customers. Second, customers feel a greater affinity for the brand because they can help shape its design. And, third, it's certainly easy to understand the economic benefit of navigating the early phases of prototype development in a virtual—as opposed to physical—environment.

Starwood's CEO, Frits van Paasschen, and its Chief Brand Officer, Phil McAveety, have lofty expectations for Aloft (an offshoot of the well-known Starwood W Hotel, targeting younger travelers with style and technology) and believe that the customer co-creation model they leveraged will make customer trial and acceptance that much more of a sure bet. By the time this book is published, Aloft will have opened dozens of new hotels. One of our favorite quotes on the early success of Aloft comes from an August 2008 *New York Times* article by Bernstein: "If the design-savvy retailer Target opened a hotel, this is what it would look like." That is a compliment of the highest form for Starwood.

The Power of Employee Co-Creation

Employee co-creation, of which earlier examples include GE, Cargill, and others, is starting to become an innovation best practice. The assumption is that employees are one of the richest yet most untapped sources of inspiration available. And why not? They are often closest to the customer and can bridge the divide of what the customer needs and what the company provides; they are generally more than willing to share their points of view if asked; and, from a pride and ego perspective, they want to see their companies succeed. Clearly companies should seek additional sources for inspiration beyond their employee base, but by not tapping into this rich pool of insights and depth of experience, they may be missing out on ideas that are sitting right in front of them (or tucked away in a file drawer in the office next door). Model Innovator companies and Visionary Marketers habitually and instinctively look to their employees as an important source for innovation. Tangible examples of employee co-creation are Best Buy and IBM.

Internal/External Co-Creation

Best Buy Robert Willett, Best Buy International's CEO, says that a huge part of the chain's success is due to frontline employees: the people who engage with customers every day. According to CMO Barry Judge, "When we ask the question of how to better thrill and motivate our customers in the store, it's the front line that can see the things that we just can't see here at headquarters."

Best Buy actively solicits ideas from its employees and uses its Blue Shirt Nation to help facilitate this process. In fact, the concept for one of Best Buy's most successful recent innovations, the technical support-oriented Geek Squad, was initiated in the field. Customer complaints about disappointing support services for PCs had spurred the employee suggestion, and Best Buy's leadership team believed it was worth investing. Today fourteen thousand Geeks are doing five thousand remote diagnostics per day at customer locations in the United States, Canada, and Europe.

IBM On November 14, 2006, IBM released this to the press:

> BEIJING, CHINA: IBM Chairman and Chief Executive Officer Samuel J. Palmisano today announced that the company will invest $100 million over the next several years to pursue ten new businesses generated by InnovationJam, an unprecedented experiment in collaborative innovation. The largest on-line brainstorming session ever, InnovationJam brought together more than 150,000 people from 104 countries, including IBM employees, family members, universities, business partners and clients from 67 companies. Over two 72-hour sessions, participants posted more than 46,000 ideas as they explored IBM's most advanced research technologies and considered their application to real-world problems and emerging business opportunities.

"Collaborative innovation models require you to trust the creativity and intelligence of your employees, your clients and other members of your innovation network," said Palmisano. "We opened up our labs, said to the world, 'Here are our crown jewels, have at them.' The Jam—and programs like it—are greatly accelerating our ability to innovate in meaningful ways for business and society."

Here are some highly successful new products and services that have come out of recent jams:

- *Smart health care payment systems:* Overhauling health care payment and management systems through the use of small personal devices such as smart cards that will automatically trigger financial transactions, the processing of insurance claims, and the updating of electronic health records
- *Intelligent utility networks:* Increasing the reliability and manageability of the world's power grids by building in intelligence in the form of monitoring, control, analysis, simulation, and optimization
- *Simplified business engines:* Developing and bringing to market an intuitive, easy-to-use, and prepackaged set of Web 2.0 services and blade server offerings that allow small and midsized businesses to easily tap applications customized to their own business needs

In addition to "jamming" now being an ongoing part of IBM's innovation efforts, the company offers its "jamming" technology to other corporations such as Eli Lilly and Nokia to harness the power of their employees and other close-in stakeholders.

The Results of Co-Creation Do you think customer and employee co-creation results in added complexity that slows down the innovation process? Not only is the answer no, in fact, when done right, such collaboration helps speed the time to market. "Together, work is completed faster and decisions are made faster. All parties—from customers to consumers to employees—are involved from the beginning, and no one needs to be 'presented' or sold to," says John Nottingham. And Nottingham certainly appreciates the importance of speed to market: "We try to compress time. Motion is progress—it's a relentless dash to the finish line."

These examples suggest that Visionary Marketers need to own managing the process of extending the reach of inspiration beyond the four walls of the organization. After all, as with customer intimacy and inspiration, access to external networks both formally and informally, internally and externally, has to become part of the Visionary Marketer's overall toolbox, especially when it relates to bringing a pervasive innovation mind-set to life.

Competencies and Cultural Dynamics Required to Win

Your organizational reality—your people, assets, leadership styles, capabilities, strategy, and firm performance—will either impede or enable a pervasive innovation mind-set to take hold. Visionary Marketers should work toward four organizational enablers of pervasive innovation success:

1. Clarity in innovation strategy and leadership
2. Supportive organizational design and culture
3. Enhanced skills, knowledge, and competencies
4. Required tools and processes for success

Clarity in Innovation Strategy and Leadership

Without the right type of leadership at the top through Visionary Marketers, the CEO, and the rest of the C-suite, innovation efforts will continue to disappoint relative to misaligned expectations and underperforming returns. While verbal, financial, and human resource support and leadership are all critical to consistent longer-term pervasive innovation success, those who are trying to

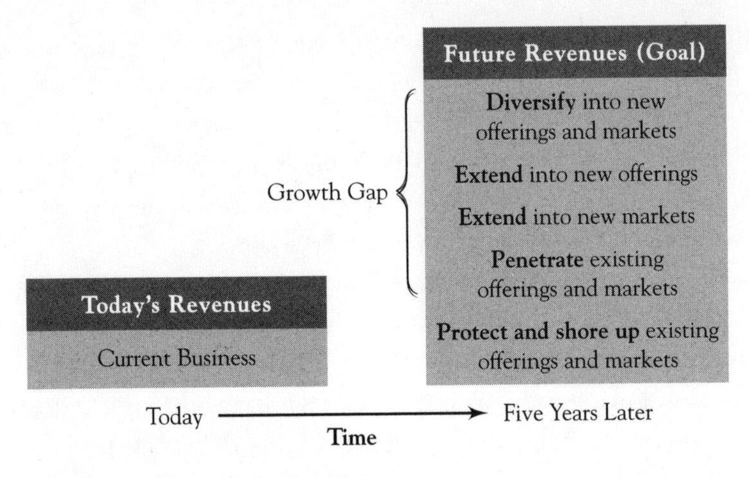

Figure 3.3 Financial Growth Gap

institutionalize innovation into their strategic lexicon and planning process would be well served to provide the strategy for how they see innovation contributing to the bottom line. As suggested in the top twelve strategic growth topics set out in Chapter One, one of the most valuable tools Visionary Marketers can leverage in helping their company make *The Shift* is to create a strategic financial growth gap, specifically highlighting the role the executive team believes innovation and other growth initiatives should play in helping the organization reach its growth aspirations (Figure 3.3).

Supportive Organizational Design and Culture

Model Innovator companies realize that pervasive innovation will succeed only if it is not limited to a single individual, function, or division. At Staples, "Innovation cuts across the company. Philosophically, every executive and employee needs to believe that they own innovation," says CMO Shira Goodman. Model Innovator companies see the power of attacking innovation issues with a distributed, cross-functional approach. When they do centralize the team, it still tends to consist of cross-functional members, often with a Visionary Marketer playing a central role.

In addition, leaders within Model Innovator cultures ensure that their employees are engaged throughout the organization and live by an ideology that ensures that pervasive innovation thrives on a daily basis. Not only do they understand, believe, and live the strategy, but their day-to-day activities and initiatives support the strategy. The culture includes openness to innovation and change, plus a tolerance for risk. It fosters curiosity, encourages risk taking, and provides the training, time, and space for employees to participate in the innovation process. Importantly, in Model Innovator companies, employees' annual MBOs (Management by Objective) and reward systems are highly aligned.

One of Google's nine points of innovation is "to allow employees to pursue their dreams," an articulation of an ideology that has fueled many of the breakthrough ideas being launched on a regular basis, including Google News, Google Suggest, AdSense for Content, and Orkut. Google's engineers are free to pursue projects they're passionate about 20% of their time. Google News was developed because one of its researchers visited ten to fifteen news sites daily to keep up with the unfolding story of the terrorist attacks on September 11. He decided to write a program to do the hard work for him, using a Web crawler to cluster articles. He e-mailed it around the company, and its potential was immediately spotted. It became a great product. As one executive says, "He didn't intend to build a product, but accidentally gave us the idea for one." That's the reason for the 20% time rule: "We trust [our people] will build interesting things."

In some organizations, Model Innovators provide employees with financial incentives if they contribute. As mentioned, American Express, according to Jim Blann, "encourages its employees to submit proposals for innovation, which are then evaluated and prioritized. The winners are then allocated a portion of a centrally managed Innovation Fund to fund their ideas." In the end, Model Innovator companies make time and space for innovation efforts, inspiring and involving everyone who can help truly build a pervasive innovation environment. To demonstrate the value of employees and their ideas, Model Innovators foster employee curiosity, encourage risk taking, and provide them with the training and the time and space to participate in the innovation process.

Enhanced Skills, Knowledge, and Competencies

To maximize the organization's innovation productivity, executives must invest in building the skills and capabilities required for sustainable, profitable growth. This also requires that you clearly know what you do and do not have in terms of your innovation inventory. You need in-depth understanding of available resources, skill sets, innovation aptitude, past success and failure factors, and the ability to know precisely what is needed to succeed going forward.

GE's unique learning culture and boundaryless organization make it another great example of a company that continues to focus on building its employees' overall skill set in service of building a pervasive innovation mind-set. To support its learning culture, GE invests $1 billion annually on education, training, and skill building for employees across the organization. There are no limits on who can generate great ideas for the business. A core philosophy is to involve everyone and welcome great ideas from everywhere. Ideas are the currency of leadership: "The hero is the person with a new idea." Importantly, as discussed throughout this chapter, GE values the application of these skills to innovation in its broadest sense: from new products to new services to new business models to new segments to pursue to new channels to leverage, and Marketing is generally in the center of the innovation wheel.

Other great examples of companies or institutions that are taking skill and competency building to the next level are these:

- Dyson, a U.K.-based vacuum cleaner manufacturer that is fully committed to innovation knowledge building and skill development for all of its employees, will open The Dyson School of Design Innovation in 2010 aimed at offering practical programs in engineering, design, and enterprise to young, aspiring innovators. The school reinforces Dyson's brand as an innovator and thought leader and enables Dyson to create and tap into a fresh pool of innovation talent.

- The MIT Enterprise Forum builds connections to innovation and technology entrepreneurs and to the communities in which they reside.
- A number of companies are hosting innovation idea exchanges, such as HP and Hallmark, while others are "swapping employees," such as the recent P&G and Google swap so people build skills by immersing themselves in each other's organizations.
- Wharton, Stanford, Berkeley, the University of Chicago, and other top educational institutions all have workshops, shorter seminars and longer programs and even centers for innovation and entrepreneurship, available to teach entrepreneurship, creativity, innovation, and/or design skills.

Required Tools and Processes for Success

Model Innovator companies have gone well beyond typical process approaches such as stage-gate and the like. They are more likely to use sophisticated tools that bring customers into the innovation process in more meaningful ways. New tools for customer interactions are surfacing regularly, and many of them leverage the power of technology and the Internet to accomplish tasks that were previously impossible.

One such tool, Kluster, is designed to harness the power of community collaboration. By offering a set of sophisticated project management tools, Kluster enables crowds to develop new concepts on behalf of participating businesses. It can be used to create products and services, plan events, or for virtually any other project that would benefit from crowd input.

Another online community-based tool is Communispace. The company has created and managed over five hundred private online communities for major corporations to deeply engage with their customers. One client was Kraft when it was considering building a weight loss and management product line based on the South Beach Diet. Kraft worked with Communispace to build an online consumer community that enabled co-creation of a line of forty-eight South Beach Diet branded products that became a $100 million success story in its first six months. Communispace works in the business-to-business world as well. CDW, a $7 billion reseller of technology products, relies on communities as the nerve center and R&D lab for its Customer First program, a companywide, cross-functional initiative to coordinate and continuously improve the customer experience. Mark Gambill, CDW's CMO, states that "Community members are generating new ideas and providing us with regular feedback and input, collectively creating the service experience, and driving the innovation that increases customer loyalty, advocacy, and word of mouth."

The popular LifeDev blog recently posted a list of "25 tools for capturing ideas," anytime, anywhere. A few additional tools listed included the Moleskine Notebook, Google Docs, and Jott, all recently developed new and improved ways of capturing any ideas, at any time, and capable of keeping an ongoing log of those ideas.

Visionary Marketers will find the right innovation tools and processes most applicable to their own situation to help build the right skill sets and competencies to win . . . and then release them to all employees to help them build a truly pervasive innovation culture.

Figure 3.4 shows how all four of these enablers work together in the broader pervasive innovation context to organize for success.

Figure 3.4 Organizing for Pervasive Innovation Success

Fusing Visionary Marketing and Innovation

Clearly the shift from incremental improvements to pervasive innovation is a journey, not an all-or-nothing leap. It has been illuminating and inspiring to see Visionary Marketers discover their role in bringing pervasive innovation to life within their company. The primary steps that aspiring Visionary Marketers need to make live within their domain and capability set. There are three steps, highlighted in Figure 3.5.

Become a Customer Zealot

As stated throughout *The Shift*, Marketing should continue to lead the charge in building a customer-centric mind-set within the

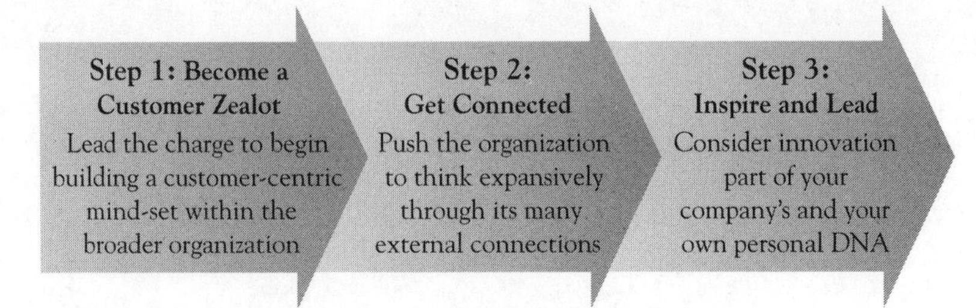

Figure 3.5 Three Steps to Pervasive Innovation

broader organization. Visionary Marketers can easily make the case that Marketing is uniquely qualified to aggregate information resources, fill customer knowledge gaps, synthesize and analyze information, and develop a customer-centric philosophy and mind-set throughout the organization.

To know how to develop a customer-centric mind-set, you must know how ready your organization is to go out and find the white space, find the insights, and find the opportunities to win with their most attractive customer segments. Some basic data-oriented questions can help you determine how ready you are to be pervasive in your approach to innovation:

- Are your data, particularly your customer data, well organized and have insights been pulled out of that data?
- If thoughtful insights have been generated, can they provide the foundation for future inspiration?
- If you have the foundation for future inspiration, are you ready to act and are customers ready to respond?

Remember that as a Visionary Marketer, you do not need to have a multimillion-dollar research budget to raise your game on becoming a customer zealot. Begin to spend more time in the field with customers and prospects and less time in the office "talking among yourselves." Listen carefully to what those in the field are telling you, follow up extensively with probing questions, and observe relentlessly. This is all a part of becoming a customer zealot.

Get Connected

Marketing, with its control over many of the external connections of the company, should push the organization to think expansively and innovate pervasively. Make a list of the people and organizations with whom your company has relationships. Everyone is fair game—suppliers, distributors, vendors, customers, competitors, consultants, and agencies. Chances are if they're in your network for one reason or another, they're also a potential candidate worth considering for partnership in innovation.

Within these connections, Visionary Marketers will thrive in their quest for inspiration. But think creatively about ways you can partner with connections, whether by formal alliances or merely turning to them as an added resource or thought partner. Think about ways in which your partnership with them can be mutually beneficial. In this day and age of accelerated networking, chances are they're also seeking the same end goal and will welcome the overture.

Inspire and Lead

Visionary Marketers must begin to consider pervasive innovation as part of their personal DNA and agenda, as well as the company's. If you're one of the fortunate few who have responsibility for the innovation agenda, great! However, if you do not, this does not mean you need to switch functions, wrestle away ownership that currently belongs to someone else, or get a promotion. As has been discussed throughout *The Shift* and will be talked about in detail in the Fifth Shift, leading through influence and collaboration, as opposed to command and control, is as powerful an approach to innovation leadership as you will find. Employees are looking to be inspired, they are looking to be taken on a journey, and they want to do their part to help exceed customer expectations. Visionary Marketers are well suited to take on this challenge!

Pervasive innovation is not a fad; it's here to stay. Other leaders, regardless of their functional orientation, are realizing the importance of growth through organic innovation. The ideal is that all leaders make it part of their personal DNA and agenda, with Visionary Marketers stepping up first.

So, What Do I Do on Monday Morning?

Here are things to consider as you think about shifting your organization from an incremental improvement to a pervasive innovation mind-set:

1. Assess where you and your company are in terms of going to market in an incremental improvement orientation versus an orientation that is more pervasive. Is innovation stuck in a silo? Is it defined by new products or line extensions, or as a way to constantly reinvent the business?
2. Have a clear understanding of why innovation, at its broadest level, has or has not taken hold in your organization and what the missing ingredient is for pervasive success going forward.
3. Create a financial growth gap clearly articulating what the growth aspirations of the organization are, as well as what the role of innovation, at its broadest level, is chartered with playing to help fill that growth gap.
4. Relative to the growth gap and broader strategic priorities, help your company articulate a point of view on what pervasive innovation could help the company achieve in service of its growth aspirations.
5. Assess where your organization is in terms of effectively leveraging the different sources of inspiration, internally and externally, to help drive innovation efforts forward.
6. Begin to create internal and external linkages, starting small, with influencers you think can best help you start to source ideas that matter.

7. Implement your company's version of an innovation jam, eliciting ideas from all pockets of your organization. And make sure you set up a safe environment where risk taking is encouraged.
8. Celebrate small and big innovation successes, as well as failures, to help perpetuate the idea that pervasive innovation is never ending.
9. Make sure you are helping to provide the tools, processes, and skills to help make pervasive innovation a way of life within your company.
10. Get going. Start small, and recognize that you are on an innovation journey. Pick a geography, a line of business, a functional area, or a category, and start pervasively innovating. You'll be surprised how early innovation wins can begin to change the culture.

Now that you have seen how Visionary Marketers can help fully leverage their network to drive influence, innovation, and companywide change, we next show how the Visionary Marketers can help the organization look at all of the marketing levers it has at its disposal, to both acquire and retain customers, over the long haul, where managing marketing investments is no longer the goal but inspiring marketing excellence is. This is about the Fourth Shift, from managing marketing investments to inspiring marketing excellence.

4

THE FOURTH SHIFT

From Managing Marketing Investments to Inspiring Marketing Excellence

Redefining the Idea of Marketing

A diversified financial services company permanently changed how it approached marketing at its broadest level, and by doing so, it made marketing excellence a source of competitive advantage.

Worried about its declining market share across its five core regions, which represent a large portion of its business, the company tried a variety of its usual tactics to try to stop the bleeding: pricing actions were planned, the marketing group developed additional promotions, and changed its product messaging, PR was thrown into the mix, and traditional advertising in TV and print was beefed up. However, there was trepidation that all that might not be enough. Frustrated and knowing the company had to get this right, and quickly, the SVP of Marketing sold the CEO on a different approach: integrating various promotional and pricing options, in different combinations, over different time periods, in an experimental design. They tracked results over a few quarters and found that the Senior Vice President of Marketing's hunch was right. The results highlighted the value of integrated marketing: pricing moves had a dramatically stronger effect when combined with promotion (direct mail and radio specifically) and PR.

The SVP of Marketing and CEO together began to understand the value of manipulating the different marketing levers they had at their disposal to change in-market results. Interestingly, they found that the primary lever the company historically depended on, price changes, most effectively changed perceptions (and ultimately sales) when combined with promotions and product messaging adjustments specific to a region. Moreover, pricing perceptions (whether customers perceive the company's pricing as being above, at parity, or below the competition) had almost as much impact on business results as the actual pricing levels.

Over the next several quarters (and years), this company continued to enhance its understanding of the optimal "Big M" marketing approach (which looks at enterprisewide growth strategies and not just marketing communications strategies [see Figure 4.1]) through subsequent analyses, each time adding new data and information to better inform the power of each offering combination. It continuously tested, controlled, experimented, and learned more about what worked and what did not and adapted accordingly.

The results were increased revenues, stabilized market share, better customer perceptions, and a turnaround in the five core regions. Another result was the elevation of the SVP to the senior executive table, working alongside the CEO to decide not only which business levers to pull and the optimal mix to secure new customers, but which longer-term company strategy made the most sense. The CEO and this Visionary Marketer ultimately worked together to transform the entire idea of marketing: from just thinking about

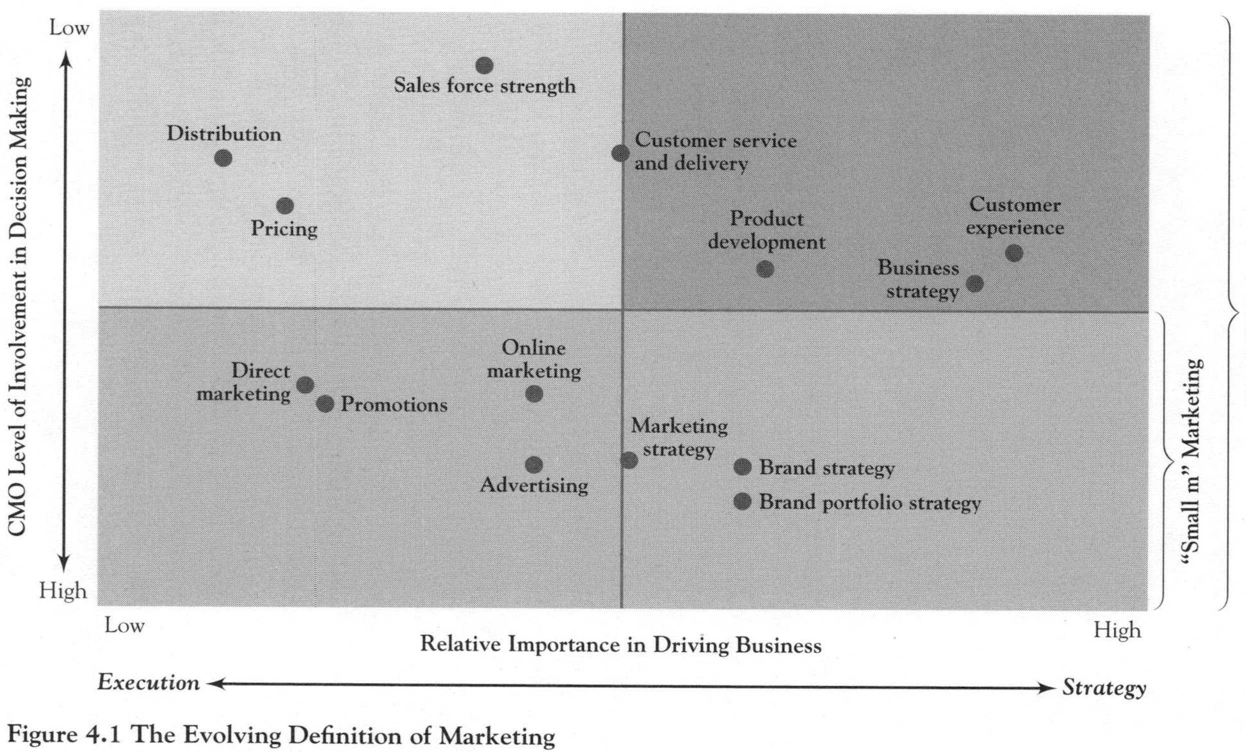

Figure 4.1 The Evolving Definition of Marketing

one aspect of traditional marketing, marketing communications, to thinking through the budget and execution against all of Kotler's 4 P's, in a Big M way and the commensurate impact this had on the overall growth agenda.

How did this come about for this company? Was it driven by crisis or by simply choosing a fresh approach? Probably a bit of both. Like so many others, this company was no longer satisfied with traditional marketing mix modeling and marketing effectiveness efforts of working with single marketing levers at a time, incomplete data sources, an ability to only look backward and broken measurement processes. It wanted and needed something better—something different from what it had experienced in the past. It wanted marketing excellence: maximizing the entire go-to-market offering and approach to maximize its marketing, selling, and overall winning efforts. This is the essence of the Fourth Shift: from managing marketing investments to inspiring marketing excellence. This shift, which is highlighted through the example above, is tied to the idea that going forward, Visionary Marketers will be interested only in maximizing the investments made across all the marketing levers (Big M marketing) and will no longer tolerate or find useful, on its own, just focusing on marketing communications (or Small M marketing). This mind-set shift is brought to life best by Barry Judge, CMO of Best Buy, who elegantly sums up what this shift is really all about in a head-on manner: "No one is interested anymore in just seeing awareness levels or only return on investment for our communications efforts. They want to hear ideas about how to help double the size of the company and what role Marketing and all functions will play in getting there!" For this to become a reality, marketers will need to move beyond just working on, looking out for, and protecting their traditional marketing agenda and budget. Visionary Marketers instead need to move forward with an expansive mind-set that encompasses the entire growth budget, agenda, and charter. This is why marketing excellence, growth, and accountability go hand in hand for Visionary Marketers.

Marketing Excellence, Growth, and Accountability

Marketers are now exposed, internally and externally, in ways they have never experienced in the past. All functional areas are under increased pressure to show results, but none is under more pressure to do so than Marketing. Marketers can no longer sit on the sidelines, doing what they have traditionally done and watching as others transform their go-to-market approaches. The Visionary Marketers interviewed for *The Shift* recognize their responsibilities inherent in this new market context:

- Mark Waller, Senior Vice President of Marketing and Sales for the NFL, agrees and adds, "I am responsible for strategic thinking within the C-suite—and for executing a plan based on that thinking across all growth drivers and levers."
- Stephen Quinn, CMO at Walmart, uses a foundation of sophisticated analysis across all Marketing levers, "which allows Walmart to only focus on programs that help the CEO get the job done for our customers and owners and to generate growth."
- Paul Ballew, Senior Vice President of Marketing Strategy and Analytics for Nationwide, notes, "Today, Marketing drives the growth agenda, along with the CEO and our board of directors. In fact, our head of corporate strategy reports to the CMO today, a visible and tangible sign that Marketing should be driving the agenda."
- Chris Gibson, CMO of UnitedHealthcare, says, "When I think of Marketing I think across Kotler's 4 P's: price,

> product, promotion, and place [distribution] because I measure my success as not only achieving Marketing results like increased leads, but also increased business sales and overall business impact."

Marketers understand that they need to become more accountable for growth, and with this accountability comes the need to demonstrate measurable results: increasing revenues, increasing market share, stronger brands, and increasing profit margins. To get these results, as highlighted in the Introduction, it is no longer enough to demonstrate depth of understanding of consumer insights alone. As noted in Chapter One, marketers need to operate with (and demonstrate) a P&L mind-set, always in service of business impact because the organization needs them to and because CEOs and CFOs will demand it.

Why Marketing Must Change Now

Several challenges and trends are driving the C-level demand for *The Shift* to hardball accountability and results from Marketing and a greater need to show where the money is going. This may be problematic for Tactician Marketers who generally focus solely on traditional marketing communications activities, as this will fundamentally challenge their orientation around being more tactically oriented as opposed to the Visionary Marketer's more strategic orientation. Some important challenges and trends will force these changes.

An Accountability Mandate

The first and foremost challenge is that Marketing must simply (or finally) face the same accountability challenges every other function does. For too long and in too many ways, Marketing has been a function without the discipline of required results. Hiding behind the guise of brand building, marketers have accumulated enormous sums of money to spend on a set of goals mostly lacking hard-core metrics tied to them. Those goals (for example, awareness levels and "intent to purchase" scores) stop several levels away from measurable in-market returns.

What other business function can do that? When was the last time the CIO was given $75 million to spend upgrading the software platform without the CEO demanding that it show a substantial return on investment? Or when are major investments in Information Technology, Human Resources, Finance, or Operations not accompanied with a business plan, set of expectations, and an idea of return or NPV? As Paul Ballew says, "Marketing investments in financial services has grown fivefold in ten years, with major firms spending upwards of 5% to 6% of revenues on marketing. . . . Is it any wonder that CEOs and Boards are asking, 'Is all this spending having an impact? Is it generating a return?' Shouldn't I be able to compare expenditures across the company tied to their expected ROIs?" To Ballew's point, the days of leaving these questions unanswered are numbered. And due to the recent global economic downturn, the need to do more with less will continue to become the operating norm.

The Differentiation Challenge

Another challenge constantly pushing marketers to have their dollars work harder for them is the increased competitive intensity and lack of product differentiation across categories. They are forcing companies (and marketers) to get their go-to-market approach right sooner rather than later, regardless of which of Kotler's 4 P's are being invested in. Signs of this pattern are unfolding in every industry: product differentiation blurs to parity among competitors, which then forces each company to become reactive instead of proactive. Commoditization rules, which forces a continual reevaluation of the Big M marketing mix. Just like pervasive innovation has to become a part of the Visionary Marketer's DNA, so does the need to continuously seek both differentiation and relevance.

Availability of Increasingly Sophisticated Measurement Tools

An important trend pushing the need for change now is the increasing ability of marketers to be able to measure the results of both individual and integrated sets of marketing initiatives on growth. An obvious cause of this increased sophistication is the rise and importance of the Internet. In the past, direct mail was the only primary direct response marketing vehicle. Today the web's ability to instantly track, report, and measure the effectiveness of advertising has increased the pressure on more traditional marketing vehicles. The increasing sophistication in measuring tools has led to a direct increase in the expectations for results, creating a virtuous circle for most companies (and a vicious circle for those that can't keep up with the improved systems).

The reality is that most marketers today are very good at tracking their individual tactical activities. For example, in a specific geography, if you lower price on a product or service, you can almost guarantee that revenues will increase. You send out a direct mail piece and receive a set of responses commensurate with historical results. You place an ad with Google, and you can measure the click-through. Such individual actions achieve quick results and are easy to measure. Nevertheless, they often tell an incomplete story, and they rarely provide insight into long-term, game-changing wins.

Across categories and industries, companies are investing millions (at times billions) of dollars to become more sophisticated with the tools and technologies available to help them finally and accurately measure impact on dollars spent. These companies generally have Visionary Marketers in the C-suite and readily use customer information, analytics, and insights to compete more effectively on a day-to-day basis. From intermediated businesses to direct-to-consumer or web businesses, this trend is driving the need for enhanced and better information, systems, and processes—all of which are driving Marketing to change its game.

A good example of these advanced measurement systems are those leveraged at Capital One and Harrah's, which allow for tracking the impact of combined or coordinated program movements, which directly measures the totality of their impact on revenues, market share, margins, and the like. Succeeding with such advanced systems requires the resources, knowledge, capabilities, and mind-set in place to fully leverage its potential.

An Action Orientation

With the greater ability to measure comes the increased responsibility to take action more quickly. An action-oriented marketing skill set helps to address such nebulous questions as: Which brands should get investment capital? Which geographies or customer sements should get less (or more) attention? Which tactics should we employ? Should we turn off the traditional marketing levers? As performance pressure intensifies, Visionary Marketers will expand their role in creating world-class marketing programs and ensuring continuous, flawless in-market execution. For this to truly work, an ongoing test-and-learn mind-set has to be in place, as discussed later in the chapter.

The Demand for Measurements and Metrics That Matter

Another important trend ties to the increased pressure to get to the measures that are specific to the individual company's requirements, rather than relying on industry standards or conventional norms. Successful Visionary Marketers strive not only to take action and get results, but also to choose the right set of metrics for the company to gauge success. They are fluent enough with the business and the company's growth objectives to understand and drive towards the best measures for the enterprise (market value, price-to-earnings ratios), the business (sales, market share, profitability), the brand (brand equity, price premiums, value), and marketing investments (vehicle return on investment, customer lifetime value, loyalty). Tactician Marketers often rely on tracking studies and other top-of-the-funnel, awareness-driving metrics, which are very hard to link to in-market results. Visionary Marketers rely on the business metrics, and their senior management counterparts rely on those that directly correlate to growth.

Directionally Correct Is Okay!

The new reality is that these trends and challenges for marketers are here to stay. They need to become ingrained operating philosophies if marketers want to move from managing marketing investments to inspiring marketing excellence. Visionary Marketers are starting to recognize that within all these challenges, a new decision-making mind-set must emerge. CMOs must learn to embrace the notion that directionally correct marketing actions might have to become the norm if they are going to keep up with all of the other challenges outlined in this chapter. The 60% plus idea that Russ Klein of Burger King discussed earlier is the mind-set; acceptance of this mind-set will come only with a consistent focus on bringing to market new ideas and programs that seem to be in line with both the company goals and what customers want. This also needs to be complemented with an entrenched, rapid-fire ability to test, learn, and adapt.

If marketers can embrace these challenges and trends, the new decision-making perspectives, and implications thereof, they will solidify their leadership positions within their organization and start to move from being Tactician Marketers to becoming Visionary Marketers.

What the "Big M" Marketing Shift Requires

If Marketing is going to move toward a more strategically oriented growth agenda, a number of internal changes need to take place in the organization.

At the top of the list, the historic division between corporate and line or product marketing budget dollars has to disappear, at least philosophically. In addition, the classic divide between allocating dollars for demand generation versus brand building will disappear; companies will no longer treat marketing investments separately; hard measures will prevail; and an overall growth budget will become the norm. This, by the way, does not diminish the need to invest to build brands. It just means that even brand-building investments need to be measured and defined, relative to growth objectives and not traditional tracking objectives, as mentioned earlier.

To this point, as CMO, Ranjana Clark continued to challenge herself and her marketing team with a simple question: "How do we spend our marketing dollars more effectively in an integrated fashion—not silo by silo?" Clark was typical of a Visionary Marketer. She did not do away with brand-building campaigns. Rather, she found a different way to increase the impact of her various marketing efforts by better understanding the interplay among all marketing variables, across the entire business.

A More Sophisticated Marketing Skill Set Is Required

A strategic orientation to the future clearly requires developing a more sophisticated marketing skill set, a deep understanding of market forces, and both a strong business acumen and strategic understanding. As a result, Tactician Marketers who have built careers on traditional marketing communication skills will find their somewhat narrow specialty area needing to become part of a larger, integrated group of activities whose aim is not to increase market awareness but rather to directly contribute to growth.

This focus on growth and accountable marketing expenditures plays well to those who have skill sets tied to classic business or P&L management. For others, embracing a P&L mind-set in Marketing will require building the right team, whose members clearly understand the business drivers of growth. As Beth Comstock of GE tells it, "Since Immelt [the CEO] believed we should be responsible for top-line growth, he said, from the beginning, 'Here is the metric; now go and get it.' " Realizing she needed a business-savvy team to achieve the growth measures that Immelt suggested, Comstock developed a system for bringing marketers up to speed on these broader business management skills in order to develop and launch programs to increase growth. She says:

> In the early days, it was defining the basics of marketing [for growth]. Most of the marketers we promoted were from within GE. Then we built up a recruiting program to bring in skilled marketers from the outside as well. It is about fifty-fifty (inside-outside) now, and we have clearly evolved into a strategic arm of the business that has a deeper understanding of what it takes to win—whether that is through innovation or just a deeper understanding of market segments.

Advanced Analysis and Insight Generation Have to Become the Norm

Successfully understanding how to conduct the analysis required to measure the impact of various growth programs—and knowing what to do with the data, analysis, and insights once they are in hand—is something that Paul Ballew at Nationwide focuses on every day. He has a seat at the C-table to help drive the growth agenda, because he uniquely understands how to best measure every dollar spent, online and off-line, that contributes to the growth of the organization. Over time, he has been able to invest in the appropriate systems, data analytics, tools, and processes to elevate the role of Marketing within the company and strengthen his relationship at the CEO and board level.

Shira Goodman of Staples keeps track of "customer analytics and insights, owning the responsibility of leveraging these insights to drive the right kind of decision-making and debates across all functional areas." Goodman has gained this responsibility because Staples has created a system under which the triggers of customer satisfaction are measured in every store, with the data being sliced by days, products, customer segments, and the like. The insights from this level of data and analysis become invaluable as Goodman enters into strategic debates on what is or is not working at a shelf, store, regional, or national level. Understanding the role of analysis in developing the right strategies to compete and win more effectively has clearly begun to separate Visionary Marketers from their Tactician counterparts.

Driving to more advanced levels of analysis and insights will be a distant idea for most companies if they don't have the requisite tools, methodologies, and approaches required to take their company to the next step. Michael Dunn, CEO of Prophet and coauthor of *The Marketing Accountability Imperative*, believes that "most companies lack the sophisticated analytical tools to provide the data and insights to truly rise to the next level. . . . [They] find themselves to be either data poor, time poor, analytics poor, or capability constrained to advance to the next level."

Assume That Marketing Spend Will Be Scrutinized Like Never Before

Ballew, Goodman, and other Visionary Marketers realize that every aspect of marketing will be examined closely, and every marketing dollar spent across the organization will be analyzed for its effectiveness. This "under the microscope" mind-set change is most noticeable (and probably toughest to change) in companies used to having significant amounts of advertising spend. Within these traditional big media spenders, such as Pepsi, P&G, IBM, and AT&T, executives across the C-suite (as well as Wall Street) are sending the message that marketers in particular can no longer continue free-spending the dollar amounts historically housed within large media campaigns. Those days are over.

Instead, companies will explore alternative paths: different vehicles for different targets with different types of risk sharing with partner agencies. And marketers will strive to prove that their big (and small) ideas can be effective—before the company's money is spent. They will continue to go against the traditional grain and make their marketing dollars work smarter for them. For instance, Becky Saeger of Charles Schwab developed an online community in which Gen Xers can discuss their personal investing issues and concerns because "we've learned that it is more important to grow with vehicles that are relevant to our targets than to just add more advertising because that is what we have always done in the past."

Without a Visionary Leadership Profile, True Accountability Will Remain a Mystery

To truly own an accountability mind-set, marketers must earn a leadership profile that goes well beyond the Tactician profile described earlier. This earned leadership profile comes in several flavors. For example, Claire Huang, former CMO of Fidelity, faced the challenge of turning around Fidelity's high-net-worth business without a real budget. Huang took on the challenge by building cross-company alliances with Distribution, Information Technology, Product Development, and other functions also charged with ultimately driving sales. Working together, this newly formed alliance provided the right levels of support to increase sales by better leveraging their collective product development, distribution, service, information, and sales data to completely change Fidelity's go-to-market approach with this target. The result was that Huang doubled the business in four years and could demonstrate that about half of this growth came from efforts driven by Marketing. Her leadership profile was forever changed.

When Yvonne LaPenotiere became the Global Branding Officer for Carlson Hotels, she had a clear agenda for how she intended to boost growth and make certain that employees across the company knew "this was not just a marketing thing, but this was a business thing." Her tough-minded approach and success were made possible in part because she had the active support of the CEO, the President, and the CFO, and she continued to bring insights and smart ways to spend marketing dollars to the table to drive tangible business impact.

LaPenotiere did a few other smart things in her quest for marketer-as-advocate-for-growth position. First, she developed a portfolio of offerings—some big, some small—to look for quick wins and generate a pool of efficiency savings, which she then used to fund growth and innovation in other areas of the company. Second, she led by example by diverting traditional marketing communication funds to internal training and customer experience enhancements, proving to the rest of the organization that she was looking out for enterprisewide growth, not marketing kudos. As a result of these important steps, her leadership profile was forever changed.

The success of these CMOs shows that if you embrace *The Shift* toward accountability and impact, your Visionary Leadership profile and seat at the C-table will be secured, and, more important, your ability to help your company meet its growth targets will be maximized.

Experimentation at the Core of Success

You now understand why marketing accountability is becoming the norm and have embraced some of the mind-set shifts that have to take place. Next up is addressing the question of how you can begin to make *The Shift* toward actually inspiring and achieving marketing excellence and not just managing marketing investments.

Inherent in this challenge will be Marketing's increased ability (and requirement) to more precisely determine and predict what has the greatest in-market success potential—the right targets, the right offerings, the right communications, the right pricing, the right timing—to meet and exceed customer needs and fuel growth. Visionary Marketers can no longer simply throw out a bunch of ideas or execute against a number of tactics and hope for the best. Rather, they need to develop plans to experiment with all the *just right* components to determine which really are best at helping to drive long-term growth and which can be cast aside or downplayed.

The challenge for many marketers is that they may believe they are experimenting when, in fact, they are testing a single element of the marketing mix. Following is a representative quote of how many marketers describe their experimenting expertise: "Of course I use experimentation. I have different test and control cells for every direct mail piece I mail." And while many companies indeed have successfully honed their skills in direct mail, applying great scientific rigor to this one aspect of marketing, they most likely are missing out in driving experiments at a much greater, more macro-oriented level. Another narrow definition of marketing experimentation is when marketers conduct field tests on new product introductions. "Of course I have experimented," a marketer will argue. "I launched in one part of the world before I rolled out globally, using a test-and-learn approach." This application of test and learn may be well intentioned, but it too is limited in scope and application as only one aspect of Big M marketing is being tested: the product.

As discussed previously, marketing levers rarely work independent of one another. Therefore, it is critical to build experiments that get at the integrated effect of testing multiple Big M levers at the same time. For example, the diversified financial services company example at the start of the chapter shows that pricing and product changes almost always go hand in hand with changes in customer perceptions. Furthermore, it was proven that "the negative impact" of increased pricing actions was mitigated when combined with other marketing levers, such as product improvements. While it took multiple in-market experiments to get to these conclusions, as demonstrated by this example, an integrated, Big M effect often has a more significant impact than independent actions on their own.

Inherent in experimentation is the opportunity to find out what does not work or is deemed to be an ineffective investment, which can be as important as finding out what does work. In organizations devoted to accountable marketing, there must be a built-in readiness and acceptance to make mistakes. Becky Saeger of Schwab agrees:

> We did a test with Condé Nast. In the magazine [we] told our customers to go to www.chuck.com and give us their thoughts. We got great engagement, but it cost too much for what we got out of it. It gave us some experience, but it also cost a lot of money that we could have allocated elsewhere. Although this didn't work out for us, we needed to test it to learn the lessons.

Implementing an experimentation mind-set and trying different approaches to winning (or at times failing) with customers represents a fundamental shift for many companies that value tried-and-true, black-and-white approaches used in the past.

Taking Experimentation to the Next Level

Visionary Marketers are discovering the power of experimentation, where they embed the analytical results of the test-and-learn approach across all the marketing levers of pricing, product, distribution, sales, and promotions. Such integrated experimentation allows marketers to mimic business situations in a microcosm, in a way that is far less risky for the business. Applying advanced experimentation across Kotler's 4 P's helps move closer to the reality of how companies manage their business in the real world by varying the elements of the marketing mix and understanding how each of the levers works in conjunction with one another (Figure 4.2) yet affords the company the ability to not go "all-in" at once. What may be a challenge for companies trying to execute against a full experimentation approach is that different Big M marketing levers may sit in different parts of the organization (for example, pricing with procurement or offering with R&D). By forcing an enterprise-wide experimentation mind-set throughout the organization,

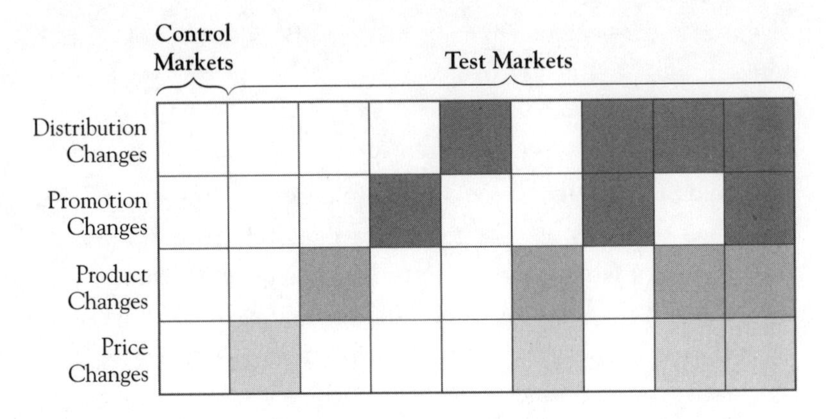

Figure 4.2 Using Integrated Experimentation

Visionary Marketers and their C-suite peers can bring to light the power of this potentially missed set of interactions, tied to a previously engrained silo mentality.

One of the most important by-products of an enterprisewide, advanced experimentation approach across multiple variables is that your organization may finally have enough data to allow the development of an in-market, marketing simulator aimed at modeling various scenarios, without having to go through a full in-market experimentation, every time. Two examples of advanced experimentation are illustrative.

In the first example, Chris Gibson of UnitedHealthcare recalls an in-market experiment that she conducted in a select number of markets with the goal of driving business growth: "We changed price, product, and place across the board and then accelerated promotional activities in some markets, which helped us prove how much changing price moved sales compared to how much additional business growth we achieved by creating the right marketing and advertising mix." Gibson notes that different combinations of print, radio, and outdoor advertising were tested, and each was linked to business goals. The resulting data proved which tactics were most effective and also "helped some of our internal business partners understand that marketing is not just communications—rather, it can be a driver of growth," she says, adding that the effort also helped UnitedHealthcare better shape its marketing investment mix: "Once we had supporting data on how to most effectively communicate our brand and benefits across a variety of tactics, we took that combination and deployed it in twenty additional markets to test its success—and it worked."

For this second example, consider the theme park operator who tried to "tactic" his way through improving the in-park experience for guests. His teams were constantly making improvements to shorten lines, improve food quality, build more exciting rides, and add more exciting shows, all in a one-off manner. What the theme park operator did not realize was that for many years, the park had built a powerful database of guest behavior trends based on making discrete moves in each park to generate higher ticket sales, park purchases, and repeat visits.

When a proven Visionary Marketer with a business background joined the park, he applied a more scientific approach to testing and controlling in-park investments. He created an advanced simulator aimed at optimizing investments in marketing (pricing moves, changes in guest experience, variations of marketing communication investments), all tied to data sources that were already being collected but in an unstructured way. So what looks like a very family-friendly, high-energy, and fun brand is actually a highly analytical, financially rigorous, experimentation-oriented company that knows how to optimize the revenue line for every guest walking through its gates. This Visionary Marketer has helped his company transform from just marketing effectiveness to ongoing marketing excellence.

As these two examples show, because growth remains the ultimate goal, Visionary Marketers should start to envision how to make the organizational changes necessary to create a culture that will consistently operate in an advanced experimental mode, have better analytics to see and interpret the results, and react faster to market changes. As noted in the UnitedHealthcare and theme park examples, the inputs and the outputs of the advanced in-market experiments conducted leveraged the entire organization, not just Marketing. With organizational buy-in and engagement, Visionary Marketers will continue to feel liberated to create new in-market experiments and simulators and use these results to continue to improve in-market results and organizational impact. In the end, advanced experimentation is as effective a basis for growth as marketers have had, but if they cannot translate the results into in-market success, then the traditional marketing jabs around Marketing's impact on business will continue to be heard.

Leveraging Test and Learn into In-Market Success

All of the sophisticated experimental design and analytics will be for naught if you do not follow through with superior in-market execution. The rich data collected across marketing variables, market dynamics, and customer segments allow finely tuned market-level guidance in what we call Marketing Playbooks.

Create Marketing Playbooks with the Details to Execute

Marketing Playbooks help guide and arm segment- or geographically-based leaders with all of the information and go-to-market approaches they need to maximize success in the segments they are trying to win. In addition, well-constructed playbooks will provide precise details on cost and return estimates tied to the mix of vehicles being leveraged as well as provide details on the precise marketing mix to apply to win with a specific target segment, given whatever unique set of market circumstances exists. These playbooks are designed much like an NFL's offensive coordinator's playbook, which spells out which play should be called given the opposing team, the defensive alignment they are showing, where the ball is on the field, and what offensive talent is at hand.

A Marketing Playbook for the Fashion World

A major women's high-end fashion company had multiple retail sites and formats, a diverse mix of SKUs and merchandise, as well as different points of view on pricing. Historically, the company had enabled each store owner to alter the mix of merchandise, price points, and hours of operation given the store's specific situation or needs. The marketers routinely collected the insights from each store but never took the application to a more sophisticated and advanced level.

A new CMO, who was a Visionary Marketer, stepped in and decided to harness all of these data sources in a structured way, working with all the marketing levers at play to test, learn from, experiment with, and control local market influence, seasonal impact, competitive responses, and other variables. This Visionary Marketer ended up creating a simulator and overall Marketing Playbook tied to the optimal mix of promotions, merchandising, pricing, and communications by location. This was all done in a way that let each store apply the simulator on its own to see what worked best for it, thus creating a customized playbook by store. This Visionary Marketer saw the opportunity to mine a rich base of data not just to alter the effectiveness of each store but to maximize the impact (and margin) of each store, leveraging all of Kotler's 4 P's, data, and insights.

Over the next few years, this CMO wants to take his advanced experimentation simulator to the next level by creating totally new customer experiences and store-within-store offerings. Leveraging the simulator in such ways should ultimately lead to an even greater impact, as well as a much more robust playbook for opening new stores. This CMO has helped his company transform from just managing marketing investments to ongoing marketing excellence success.

Regional Versus Segment-Specific Marketing Playbooks

If the company focuses on sales efforts by region, the marketer will create a regionally focused Marketing Playbook with a snapshot of the local market and the specific tactics required to succeed to generate sales. This can include the unique combination of new products, pricing, and promotion efforts, geared to that sales territory, and based on these components:

- *Competitive intensity.* Who is playing in that market with what product, price, and promotion combination?
- *Brand strength.* What incremental spend do I need to increase my current brand or product strength in a given market?
- *National versus local initiatives.* Which programs or initiatives should be executed at the corporate level, and which should have local autonomy?

As an example of the power behind generating these regional Marketing Playbooks, the diversified financial services company that opens this chapter was able to move to the next level of growth when the marketing team took the insights from the modeling experiments and developed local Marketing Playbooks, deploying them across all regions. The playbooks had two specific components. First, they included market snapshots, highlighting local market nuances specific to each geography. These would ultimately help inform different strategic development alternatives (Table 4.1). Second, they provided specific tactics tied to the requirements to win within each market. For instance, each region was allowed to buy media differently, with regional marketing executives empowered to make locally driven pricing decisions. In the same way, each locale was allowed to have a minimal number of variances, tied to new product or service introductions, as well as to adding or subtracting sales force, as needed. However, the

Table 4.1 A Market-Level Playbook Example

NORTHEAST REGION			
	Drivers of Revenue	**Market Condition**	**Market Actions**
Price	Price perceptions	Unfavorable	Immediately highlight affordability
	Actual price	Favorable	
	Price momentum	Favorable	
Product	Quality perceptions	Favorable	Prioritize new product line launch
	Breadth of offer	Unfavorable	
	Service penetration	Favorable	
Promotion	Brand awareness	Unfavorable	Make significant investment in promotions
	Share of voice	Unfavorable	
Place/ Distribution	Channel penetration	Favorable	Launch channel sales training program
	Channel satisfaction	Favorable	
	Channel growth	Unfavorable	

formula by which they would make these decisions would be the same nationally, as would be the messaging approach.

Similarly, if the company organizes around customer segments, the Visionary Marketer can slice the data by segment, providing a snapshot of the research on that segment and developing a Marketing Playbook for the customer segment level. By sharing the fact-based, experimentally tested, analytical results along with go-to-market recommendations for the different market-facing groups, the Visionary Marketer will have created a more strategic and tactical relationship with the parts of the business that help to justify marketing. This will generally include a unique combination of new products, pricing, and promotion efforts geared to a specific target segment based on the following factors:

- *Segment needs and wants*. What are the top needs, wants, frustrations, and white space opportunities for this segment? How does this match with our offerings today?
- *Segment-specific purchasing criteria*. What influences the purchase most for top segments: pricing, offering, promotions, channel? How well are we set up to win the sale against these criteria?
- *Segment specific competitor map*. How do competitors differ by segment—are they more service oriented, pricing oriented, or convenience oriented? How can we change our mix against each competitive set?

Turning Marketing Playbooks into In-Market Success

Once Marketing Playbooks are built, the next issue is integrating the inputs into actual decision-making processes, with tools such as decision trees as shown in Figure 4.3. Far too often, even if the effort to build successful Marketing Playbooks happens, the organization is not ready or equipped to react or make decisions based on the results. For example, regional Marketing Playbooks for a global mutual fund company were recently built based on months of in-market experiments. One of the major outcomes was that the company was leaving money on the table in a specific geography with a particular set of customers. The challenge became how to implement change to recoup that "lost" money. The planning processes for allocating investments was set, as was the product strategy, but pricing moves took months to get regulatory approval, and the company became

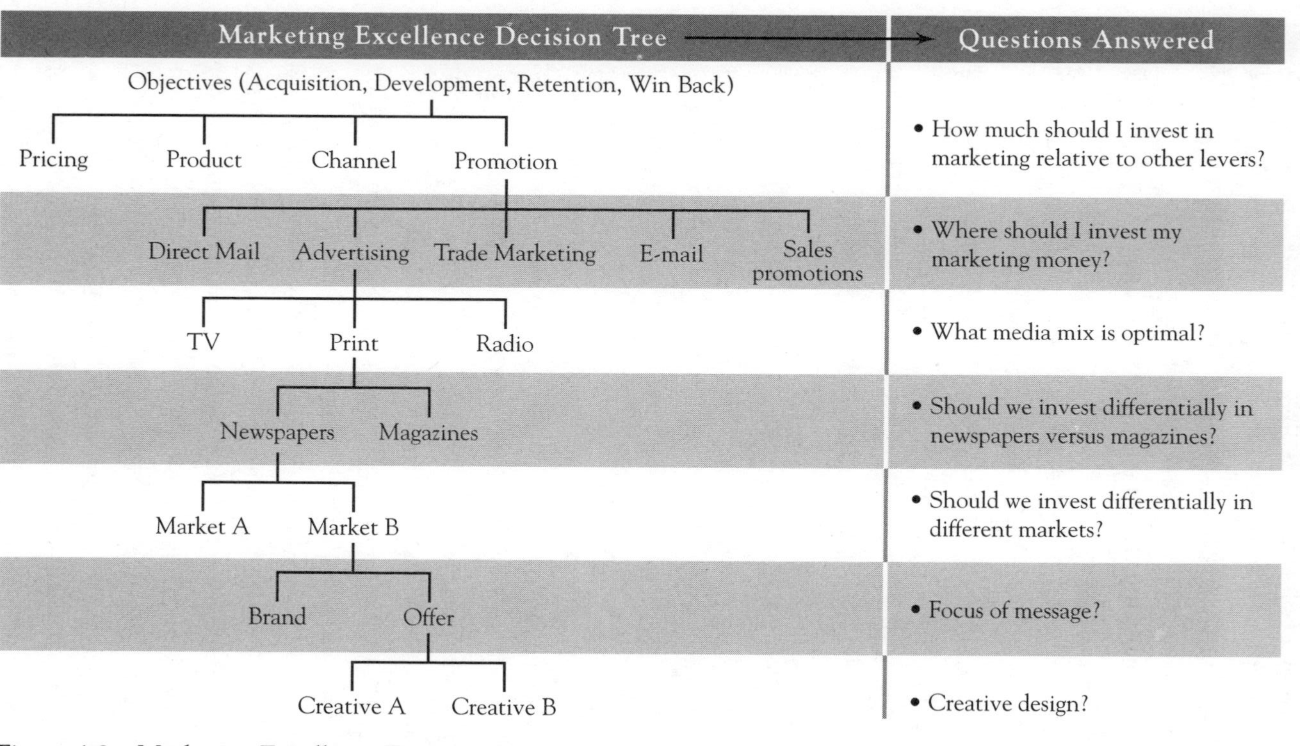

Figure 4.3 Marketing Excellence Decision Tree

handcuffed by broken or rigid processes. Marketing Playbooks need to be integrated into strategic (or annual) marketing and sales planning cycles and financial reporting processes to maximize the chances of their results turning into in-market impact.

The types of questions and the Marketing Playbooks developed for regional versus segment-specific focus may differ greatly, but the bottom line is that they provide a level of specificity for the organization, tied to the topic of what to do about specific situations that Marketing and the rest of the organization most likely have not addressed in the past. They also arguably provide the Visionary Marketer with a unique asset base that no one else in the organization has access to, across all segments. In addition, well-done Marketing Playbooks, incorporating powerful data, test results, information, and tools, will permanently change the types of dialogues marketers are having across the organization as well as the organization's in-market potential for success. They will help provide market-facing employees, such as the sales force or the call center, with the best chances for success by providing them with just what they need to close the sale and delight the customer. To go a step further, Marketing can even equip the sales force with easy-to-use tools, such as decision trees, which will allow them to change their selling approach on the fly with a high degree of accuracy.

Using the results from advanced experimentation as a guide and regional- or segment-specific Marketing Playbooks as a by-product, Visionary Marketers help to identify the business levers, independently and in combination, that will help drive business success through a well-scripted, play-by-play format. Best-in-class companies will continue to deepen their understanding of the impact of different levers of Kotler's 4 P's by integrating these natural experiments into in-market results. If all goes well, Visionary Marketers will have a virtuous circle of analysis, refined Marketing Playbooks, and enhanced results, driving not only stronger marketing outcomes but also stronger business outcomes.

A Few More Questions

Of course, there's more to sort out in the Fourth Shift from effectiveness to excellence, especially regarding overall expenditures and returns on investments made.

How Much Money Are We Actually Spending?

Visionary Marketers need, and have, the opportunity to gain a deeper, more accurate understanding and evaluation of how much money is being spent annually on marketing investments. The questions probably sound familiar: Do we really know what we spend on marketing? And what should be included? Shouldn't local sales promotions or events be included? How do we account for business unit spending versus corporate? How about digital versus nondigital or traditional versus nontraditional? Many companies lack an integrated view of their investment dollars spent. Without being able to address these questions, the upside of spending dollars more efficiently may never be known, and budget silos will remain intact.

The obvious challenge here is that many marketers do not have ready access to the data required to take on this exercise. Too often marketers find that the data sets sit in disparate systems or they can find no data history beyond a few years, or, worse yet, they may not truly know who their end customer is and therefore do not understand what they are really looking for. The silver lining in this exercise is the opportunity to reach across functions and business units to start to collect these data for the greater organization and, at the same time, start to build some alliances that will come in handy in the future.

Sean Burke at GE remembers how hard it was to take on an exercise of this magnitude:

> Early on, there was frustration, among a few junior managers here, who wanted to accomplish more in marketing,

but because we were not your traditional marketing company, it was difficult to get the discussion off the ground because the budget was just not identified—even though the organization was clearly spending money on marketing activities across the business. I challenged them to not get frustrated but to change the dialogue. I told them if they wanted to have a real talk about marketing strategy and budgets, then we would together have to have a better understanding of what we spend in marketing today in order to demonstrate there was opportunity to improve.

Fortunately, over the years, we had gained enough credibility with the senior executive team to launch an initiative aimed at better understanding total marketing spend throughout the business. Working with finance and the other business unit leaders, we pulled together all line items categorized as marketing, which totaled sixty thousand line items. We then went through (with the team) every single line item to determine where there was waste, duplication, or inefficiencies and found tremendous savings . . . that we were ultimately able to funnel back into smarter marketing investments. Along the way, our credibility and bridge building with other functions increased exponentially, as I was able to save them money and invest in programs that had a higher return on investment. And, importantly, Marketing was able to actually get accountability, for the first time, of the marketing budget!

Can We Actually Link Marketing and ROI?

In addition to marketers not always having a holistic picture of total marketing spend, they also continue to lack a singular common measure of ROI. Even in companies with good data, most senior marketing executives do not agree on the appropriate measure of ROI. Should they be measuring a true return or just improvements in sales, units, volumes, or something else? And should they be wed to a single ROI metric or rather a combination of relevant metrics?

As Tülin Erdem, a Leonard N. Stern Professor of Business Administration and Marketing at New York University's Stern School of Business, has pointed out, "managers are under more pressure than ever to justify their marketing expenditures in a much more rigorous and quantifiable way." She goes on to say:

> Measurement of marketing effectiveness is too often considered to be an exercise that involves the linking of marketing expenditures to financial metrics, such as return on investment. But I think marketing effectiveness is much broader than that: focusing on and measuring marketing effectiveness involves setting quantifiable goals and objectives (which may go above and beyond recovering your investment), measuring both the processes that underlie customer responses, as well as measuring marketing outcomes and letting this focus also guide the development and implementation of your marketing strategy and programs.

Marketing effectiveness is more than ROI: it is proving that marketing strategy is integrated with business strategy to increase revenues and ultimately profitability. Understanding the complementary nature of the different levers at your disposal, and then demonstrating how each resulting action symbiotically affects every other action, thereby increasing their effectiveness, is where Visionary Marketers can really take off. In the diversified financial services company example at the start of the chapter, the Visionary Marketer took over the controls of the entire growth engine, using a full array of capabilities to help transform the company. This SVP completely changed the perception and role of Marketing, and this company has forever changed the way it goes to market.

This is how Becky Saeger talks about ROI at Schwab: "With marketing effectiveness, which is the ROI on the entire marketing dollars of the organization, . . . we look within the portfolio of marketing activities to see the specific areas where we succeeded and failed, take stock of lessons learned and always look to better our efforts, as we continue to go to market with a much more integrated perspective. ROI and marketing effectiveness is a constant journey for us."

However, even without a perfect ROI correlation, Visionary Marketers will continue to go down varying paths to demonstrate that their programs help to drive their company's goals for growth, based on the metrics that are most important to that company's growth objectives. Moreover, the focus on returns in whatever form should not mean that Marketing should forget about the linkages of the marketing investments on traditional brand metrics: brand awareness, familiarity, consideration, perceptions. To focus on return does not mean that they should focus just on the short-term business impact. It also means they need to assess the linkage of longer-term metrics such as brand health to business outcomes. In fact, the strength of Marketing is the ability and discipline to consider both the short- and long-term impact of the broader marketing investments.

For companies that get the importance of *The Shift*, the new norm will be to drive more efficient marketing budgets and plans of attacks, while adopting an experiment-your-way-to-growth mindset. This will eventually transform the dialogue from one about marketing investments to one about marketing excellence.

So, What Do I Do on Monday Morning?

Here are things to consider in your organization as you think about shifting from managing marketing investments to inspiring marketing excellence:

1. Assess where you and your company are in terms of ability and desire to address the long-term marketing investment management to marketing excellence challenge.
2. Get a clear understanding of all marketing spend today across the 4 P's. Identify and catalogue all critical sources of marketing and business data for future use, as well as examples of market experimentation, to inform future advanced experimentation opportunities.
3. Clearly understand business priorities and how marketing investments tie to those priorities.
4. Determine if you have the analytical capabilities to conduct experimentation. Assess the marketing team skill set and the specialists still required.
5. Begin to create alliances with all groups that touch Big M marketing levers: Sales, Distribution, Product, Pricing, and so forth.
6. Look across all 4 P marketing levers to identify which initiatives would be appropriate for experimentation, and execute against a few high-impact, in-market experiments tied to the business priorities identified.
7. Begin to create either regional- or market-segment-level playbooks, leveraging cross-functional and business unit relationships.
8. Track all results, and gather data that feed into the experiments and the playbooks. Analyze the impact of marketing investments on business results expeditiously.
9. Ensure every dollar of marketing spend has its appropriate metric for success. Track brand health metrics by segment and market on a regular basis.
10. Get going. Start small, and recognize that you are on a marketing excellence journey. Pick a geography, a line of business, a

medium, or a campaign, and start measuring. (You'll be surprised how early returns can begin to change the culture.)

You have now seen how Visionary Marketers can fundamentally shift the way their organization grows by deploying all of the Big M weapons it has in its arsenal. Next, it is important to understand how best to get the organization on board, aligning all functions, business units, and the overall executive team around the customer. This is the Fifth Shift: from an operational focus to a relentless customer focus.

5

THE FIFTH SHIFT

From an Operational Focus to a Relentless Customer Focus

This book has covered a lot of ground across the first four shifts: repositioning the marketing function to have a much greater leadership profile; adopting a P&L and accountability orientation; embracing the network concept in service of an end game of knowledge-based influence, not overt control; understanding that pervasive innovation has to pervade the entire organization; and making a norm of thinking beyond marketing communications' mix modeling, through the entire go-to-market approach. Marketing has to sit at the C-table. Why? Because it can become one of the organization's greatest assets for growth.

Many other themes have emerged as well, including Visionary Marketers' ability to be known for having a responsibility, ownership, and experimentation mind-set. Visionary Marketers' ability to leverage their secret weapon of customer-led insights into every conversation relating to growth will continue to help them define their power base. So will their ability to help their organization focus on only the strategic imperatives that matter for the longer-term growth agenda.

For all this to take hold, the organization will need to shift and align, perhaps for the first time, around the concept of becoming customer led and truly having a relentless focus on the customer. Visionary Marketers will need a diverse set of tools that enable them, as well as their peers, to cross over traditional and sacred boundaries into other functions and disciplines. Collaboration needs to extend across all functional areas, and the stereotypical battles so often existing between, say, Marketing and Sales will have to disappear. The goal is to win customers, and the way forward is a fully integrated, go-to-market approach that holds Marketing, Sales, Finance, IT, Human Resources, and other units jointly accountable for the growth of the organization. Once this level of collaboration, coordination, and connectivity takes hold, magic can and will happen, both internally and externally. Just ask the Visionary Marketers at Schwab, Burger King, GE, Dell, and Apple.

Collaborating and working fully around, and for, the customer is no easy feat. Most organizations still operate under archaic organizational constructs with a functional silo mentality. For instance, too often Marketing has to convince Sales that certain segments are the most profitable to pursue and it is okay to discard the others. Information Technology has to convince Finance that a major overhaul in the customer relationship management (CRM) system is critical for Marketing to be able to provide pragmatic and useful information to the sales force. Marketing has to convince operations that a new billing system is the only approach for fixing one of its most problematic touch points. Human Resources has to convince Finance to give it the funding for a world-class training curriculum. Meanwhile, the Board is pushing all for greater accountability but using outdated metrics systems to do that essential accounting.

Through this all, the one who is pushing the hardest, the one who is the most demanding, the one who doesn't care about internal debates, politics, and turf wars, is the customer. Customers want the experience you promised, the quality levels they expect, service levels that are best in class, and an indisputable value for their money. In return, they will give you the loyalty you yearn for, the share of wallet you believe you have earned, the openness to try your latest and greatest offerings, and the forgiveness you will ask for if you make a mistake. It's quite a give-and-take—and achievable only if the organization is working in unison on delivering in a customer-led way.

You need to be all-in and relentlessly focus on your customers.

All-In at DKSH

In 2002, the Asian business of the trading firms Diethelm, Keller, and SiberHegner, was merged to form DKSH, headquartered in Zurich, Switzerland. All three predecessor companies had been in business for almost 140 years, but only the mergers gave them the scale and coverage to truly become a global player. Following the mergers, DKSH had a combined thirteen thousand employees and annual revenues exceeding $3.6 billion. It was now in a position to redefine its business model and growth aspirations. However, challenges existed.

After the mergers were completed, DKSH quickly realized that it needed more than scale to capitalize on its growth potential. Martina Ludescher, Vice President of Strategy and Corporate Communications, recalls, "As a result of the mergers, we quickly realized that we were no longer just a trading company, and thus we had to redefine what business we were in, as well as our underlying business model." If that wasn't a big enough challenge, DKSH also realized that it needed a recognized market face and a common service delivery platform to achieve its aggressive growth aspirations. In the words of the visionary CEO, Joerg Wolle, "I regularly travel around the world, meeting with clients and customers, across our businesses, almost every day of the week, and back then it became abundantly clear to me that we needed a strong brand that would help speak for me and allow me to focus more on growing the business and serving clients and customers more effectively."

So DKSH started on a journey aimed at defining an aggressive path forward—one that would drive exponential growth by both leveraging and building on their people, physical assets, and newly acquired scale. Early on, detailed market research uncovered inconsistencies in the way the brand was perceived internally and externally. The research showed that externally, this newer brand was not as well known as was believed internally. And contrary to the internal perception that DKSH should principally focus on its clients (those who are leveraging DKSH's ability to sell their products and services in Asian markets), as opposed to customers (the hundreds of thousands of outlets that DKSH serves every day), the research proved that customers were equally important stakeholders because clients seek their advice when choosing a partner such as DKSH.

The DKSH management team realized that these external gaps mirrored internal practices that continued to support separate and distinct actions rather than an integrated point of view. The DKSH management team also saw these internal and external disconnects as signs of limitations in its ability to drive increased shareholder value and overall firm growth. The business historically had been built on entrepreneurs running separate business units and operating fairly autonomously. There was little cross-selling, knowledge sharing, or recognition of DKSH as a true global brand. In fact, in the early days after the merger, clients and employees still referred to the larger enterprise by the individual entity names—Diethelm, Keller, and SiberHegner—and never by DKSH.

In 2008, six years after the merger, DKSH announced double-digit growth for the sixth year in a row, with revenues at almost $9 billion; moreover, earnings more than doubled in those six years (Figure 5.1 shows the DKSH playbook to success). Dozens of companies have been absorbed into DKSH or its predecessor companies before and after the merger. Since 2002, DKSH has acquired twelve companies across nine countries. This rapid development

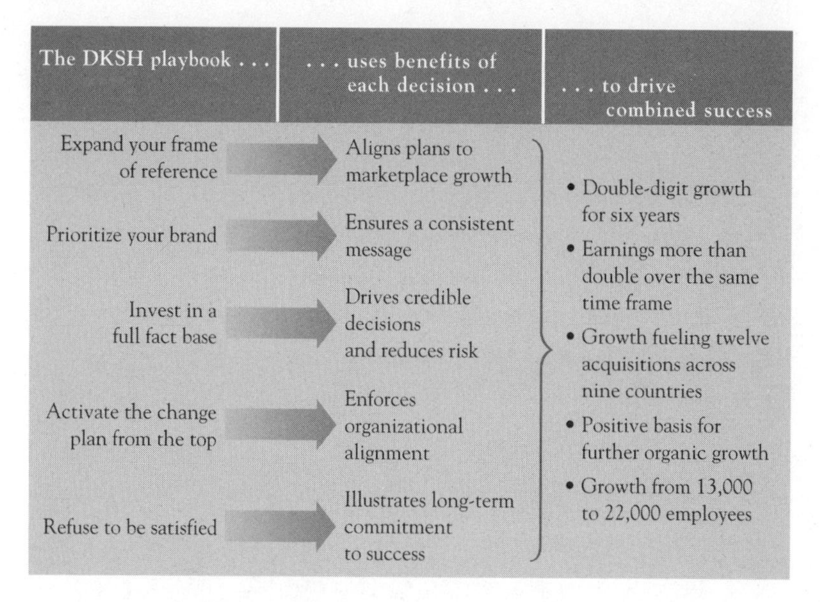

Figure 5.1 DKSH Playbook to Success

has enabled it to add new investors and a significant amount of new capital, which has created a positive basis for further organic growth, acquisitions, and other strategic investments, all while operating in an uncertain economy. This is no small feat, considering that the enterprise had grown to twenty-two thousand employees.

If you ask DKSH executives what enabled them to reach these unprecedented levels of growth in a global recessionary climate, they would tell you that they shifted from having a business unit-centric, country-based approach to having a truly market-led, relationship-driven, solution-oriented partnership with both their clients and customers. This is indicative of the Fifth Shift: moving from a company organizing itself in a traditional functional or silo-mannered approach to a company aligning itself and operating in a more customer-centered, customer-first approach, often led by a Visionary Marketer or CEO. And this is what happened at DKSH.

Not unlike IBM in the late 1990s and HP, FedEx, and Xerox more recently, Wolle and Ludescher realized that the scope of businesses that they offered and the company's frame of reference for how they were positioned in the marketplace were no longer well aligned. They redefined the company from being a trading company to what they now are calling a market expansion services enterprise, offering a comprehensive range of services that help companies enter or expand their businesses in Asia. In doing so, Wolle and Ludescher dramatically reframed the business, expanded their frame of reference, and shifted how they went to market.

The secret in making this transformation work so well had four primary ingredients critical to implementing the Fifth Shift:

- First, as Ludescher states, "Having a CEO that is intimately involved in each of the businesses and a vocal and supportive participant of Marketing has really been the key to setting the foundation for our efforts' success."
- Second, the collaboration between Wolle and Ludescher, and the rest of the executive team in taking on this repositioning effort was unprecedented at DKSH.
- Third, the voice of the client and customer led the entire repositioning dialogue.
- Fourth, the entire executive team was able to move forward with a different type of organizational context—one that is more customer and client centered and encouraged much stronger collaboration across functional areas and the entire employee base.

Ludescher believes this transformation fundamentally shifted the culture:

> We are such a diverse services company but always need to remember that the single greatest asset we have is our people and their ability to have successful interactions with our clients and customers. Being responsible for twenty-two thousand employees all using the same playbook is no small task. It requires the respect of business unit executives and the trust that our group can have an impact and help them continue to be successful.

Working in true collaborative teamwork-like fashion across functions, Marketing became a strategic voice and asset that DKSH had never fully seen or leveraged in the past. In addition, Marketing became a driver of growth, fully leveraging its ability to aggregate knowledge across regions, businesses, and customers to develop a global marketing and growth strategy, with the commensurate priorities for driving the corporate growth agenda.

Today Marketing at DKSH is responsible for the overall customer experience, making sure that the brand is being operationalized consistently in every region where DKSH competes and fully driving the strategy of which touch points the organization should focus on. Because Marketing's primary sponsor is CEO Wolle, DKSH now goes to market every single day with a truly integrated, customer-led organizational approach and an operating philosophy of "we are all in this together" to win the battle for the customer and client.

Wolle believes DKSH has not even come close to reaching its potential yet:

> Our story is only beginning. We have the right people in place, we have alignment around internal roles and responsibilities so we go to market with one voice, we are crystal clear as to what makes DKSH special and distinct, and we ensure all of our employees deliver on our client/customer promises every single day.

In effect, DKSH has totally transformed itself into being organized around the client and customer, with Marketing being a leading voice in this transformation.

The Realities of a Relentless Focus on the Customer

Philosophical shifts that manifest in different behaviors, such as the one that took place at DKSH, are major undertakings, but by no means are they out of reach for most companies. However, we caution you to move into this Fifth Shift with eyes wide open. Your company will most likely have an entrenched, historical organizational perspective and legacy approach to doing business. It may have worked well for a long time, but it may not be suited for a customer-focused transformation tomorrow.

In addition, the push for a more customer-centric, organizational transformation, led by a Visionary Marketer, may be hampered if the marketer has not yet garnered the respect from his or her organizational peers to engage in organizationwide, transformation-oriented dialogues. A recently published study, *The Evolved* CMO, by Forrester Research and Heidrick & Struggles, supports this notion through some of its key findings:

- One-quarter of CMOs are not involved in any way with customer service and support. They are distanced from what customers are saying in the field and from important internal support groups, and thus dismissing themselves from critical internal discussions taking place, revolving around the customer.
- Most CMOs said that within their organization, their relationship with the CFO is poorly developed or even nonexistent, a possible signal that Finance dismisses Marketing in many organizations.
- Marketing still controls mostly traditional communications efforts and has little engagement in the overall organizational strategy.

To further support this notion, the CMO Council's 2008 *Marketing Outlook* study named "organizational culture and senior management mind-set" as Marketing's areas of biggest internal aggravation and frustration.

So where do you go from here with this vicious circle in place: Marketing is disconnected, thus Marketing is dismissed, thus Marketing goes back into its comfort zone of being a Tactician Marketer, and thus Marketing is disconnected? How can Visionary Marketers help to start to make the Fifth Shift to a more customer-centered organizational approach and capture all of the benefits encompassed within the first four shifts, if this vicious circle remains intact? One way to start to get traction on this transformation dialogue is to borrow some ideas from the network concept introduced in the exploration of the Second Shift and move to a more collaborative, networked approach internally. Make no mistake, collaboration in service of the customer is more than "simply playing well with the other functions." It necessitates collective buy-in around the importance of operating from the customers' perspective and then driving the requisite internal actions to drive the right in-market activities to get to the desired outcome—delighted customers.

Start Working Inward from the Customer

Stop thinking about how you are organized internally, and start thinking about how the customer experiences you on both a day-to-day basis and at those critical moments of truth that often help to define the type of experience and relationship a customer ultimately has with your company. Once you start with the customer in mind and work your way back through the company's organizational structure, you will quickly see a dizzying number of organizational touch points and functions that influence the overall customer experience. You will also probably see that the organization is not truly organized for maximum success from the customer's perspective.

For instance, from a customer's outside-in perspective, there may be a billing issue that lives in Information Technology, or a call center issue that lives in Customer Service. It may be a broker issue that lives in the Sales organization or a product issue with R&D. Each of these issues can have an undeniable influence on the customer's experience with your company, product, service, or brand, and at any point, any one of these touch points could make

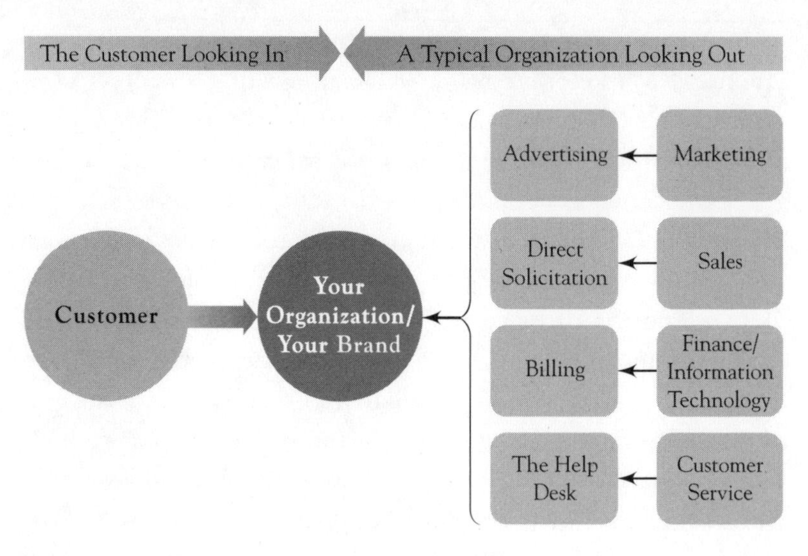

Figure 5.2 The Customer Sees One of You

or break the customer relationship. Now look at the same issue as viewed from the organization's inside-out perspective in terms of functions (Figure 5.2). Does HR, which hires all of the talent to be deployed against market opportunities, have any less responsibility for ultimately winning over the customer than does Sales? How about Finance and Pricing in making sure there is a good price-value equation for every good sold, in comparison with Customer Service, which has to handle after-sales issues? How about Marketing, which helps drive customers into the organization, versus Information Technology, which makes sure that the online experience, from sales to billing, works in a customer-centered way? How about Distribution, which has to make sure the product is at the right place, at the right time, versus R&D, which is charged with driving the next generation of offerings? Who is overseeing all of these functions to make sure they are all aligned to deliver a world-class customer experience? For most companies, that "who" is not very clear, and none of the functional areas mentioned above should be excused from operating in a truly customer-driven, customer-centered, customer-is-king way.

Another related reality is that most organizations are not equipped to deliver and win at critical moments of truth—by the customer's watch—because they are rarely organized around how the customer wants to engage with the organization. Most companies tend to organize for operational effectiveness and efficiency and are tied to approaches that work well for the organization but not necessarily for the customer.

According to the CMO Council study, mentioned previously, "Marketers must find a way to drive cross-functional alignment between the brand promise and the delivery of the brand promise at all customer touch points . . . and take the lead within the company to make sure that every function understands its role in delivering the desired customer experience . . . and it will only happen when activities are well orchestrated, managed and measured."

We could not agree more.

So the critical Fifth Shift questions (similar to those posed within the first four shifts) to address are:

- Can the Visionary Marketer take the lead role in repositioning the customer to be the center of the organizational universe, coordinating touch points and functions to deliver with a customer-first mind-set, in effect working for the customer?
- Can the Visionary Marketer help the organization rethink how it is (or is not) set up to win?

To answer these questions, you need to return to the question of control versus influence, which was discussed in the Second Shift. Should the Visionary Marketer exert control to drive customer-centered change—or exert smart influence and collaboration to accomplish these goals?

Although it may not seem as forceful when driving a true organizational shift, Visionary Marketers would be smart to use organizational influence and collaboration to help their companies start the journey of organizing around the customer. They must start at the very top and leverage an appropriate balance of collaboration, influence, and shared leadership, with the appropriate doses of vision and inspiration. This type of marketer-led influence model will induce marketers to borrow some approaches from their softer side of marketing influence: building alliances and coalitions, understanding and listening to peers' concerns and issues, engaging in dialogues and debates that provide direction rather than dissension, and bringing others into the conversation so it is an organizationwide conversation, not an insular marketing conversation.

Inspire the Organization to Align Differently

When addressing the question of organizing for the customer, a frequently asked question pertains to whether companies need a personnel, organizational reorganization, or a philosophical transformation leading to new behaviors to achieve the suggested Fifth Shift of customer-facing change. Generally, reorganizations are the by-product of cost-cutting efforts, a merger or an acquisition, or a major company overhaul. Reorganization connotes massive overhauls, lots of time, lots of brain damage, and lots of questions like, "Do we really need to?"

But organizations looking to become customer led do need a transformation and mind-set shift to help infuse a new way of thinking, a new way of operating, and fresh energy for driving customer-centric growth. The most successful, customer-led transformations succeed when they are focused on both:

- Galvanizing and inspiring the organization to align around a new and different customer-centric, go-to-market approach from the top down, inspired by senior leadership
- Ensuring internal and external clarity on the organization's positioning . . . what it is, and importantly, what it is not

Clarity Through Inspired Organizational Leadership

There are several ways to galvanize and inspire the organization to go to market in a more customer-centric way. One way is for leadership at the top to inspire those beneath them through their vision and voice. Another is to position the company in a way that is absolutely clear to customers and prospects as to what the company promises and what every customer should expect of every employee and every experience. A third way is to simply not waver from your organization's original customer-centric history—one that perhaps has always focused on meeting and exceeding customers' expectations.

Tony Hsieh, CEO of Zappos, presents a clear example of what can be accomplished through the inspiration of corporate leadership. For those lucky enough to start from scratch, this Archetype I, Instinctive Marketer, is a best practice example. Hsieh has mastered the notion of galvanizing his workforce to provide unconditional personal service to the growing legions of Zapposians. Hsieh emphatically states that Zappos' number one priority is its company culture, and this is evidenced in the ten core values that Zappos embraces to make it a better place to serve customers.

"Zappos' Ten Core Values"

1. Deliver WOW Through Service
2. Embrace and Drive Change
3. Create Fun and a Little Weirdness
4. Be Adventurous, Creative, and Open-Minded
5. Pursue Growth and Learning
6. Build Open and Honest Relationships with Communication
7. Build a Positive Team and Family Spirit
8. Do More with Less
9. Be Passionate and Determined
10. Be Humble

To adhere to these values, he says, "we have had to untrain employees' bad habits from previous call centers' and services' experiences, where they're trying to be more efficient by minimizing the time they talk to the customer. The more time we spend with customers on the phone, the deeper the relationship will be."

Thus, Hsieh's longer-term goal is clear: to create lifelong relationships with customers, which means two things for the company. First, Customer Service will always be treated as an investment, not an expense. And second, Zappos will hire people based on how well they will fit into the culture and their perceived ability to live up to Hsieh's customer service expectations.

Not surprisingly, Zappos is on *Fortune's* "Best Companies to Work For" list.

> The company's [2009] debut at No. 23 makes it the highest-ranking newcomer on the list. . . . For nearly ten years the online retailer has sold shoes and, increasingly, apparel and electronics to fawning customers who love the policy of free shipping in both directions. Zappos is also adored by employees, providing a model of how to manicure culture and treat staffers like adults, while simultaneously reassuring them that sometimes it's okay to behave like children.

Interestingly, this effort to build a motivated, impassioned culture paid off in a somewhat unexpected way when Zappos was faced with the economic situation of 2008, and found itself, like so many other companies, having to lay off employees.

As the *Fortune* article explained:

> Hsieh wanted to get the news out fast to mitigate stress. He announced the move in an e-mail, on his blog, and with Twitter. . . . The Internet can be a hostile place,

> but the blogosphere and the Twitterati had a surprisingly positive reaction to the way the downsizing was handled. . . . Laid-off employees with less than two years of service would be paid through the end of the year. Longer-tenured staffers would get four weeks for every year of service. Everyone would receive six months of paid COBRA health coverage. At the request of departing employees, Zappos also allowed them to maintain the 40 percent employee discount through Christmas. Says Hsieh, "The motivation was, let's take care of our employees who got us this far."

As another example of leading from the top, in an interview with CMO *Magazine*, Jim Stengel (now retired Visionary Marketer at P&G) brought to life what A. G. Lafley meant when he pushed P&G to become more customer-centric. Stengel stated, "Becoming more customer-centric does a couple things. It gives us more aspirational and strongly defined brands. It also has a tremendous effect on the culture because it gets people out of the office and working together in unexpected situations. It galvanizes teams on what's really important." Stengel went on to admit that one of the biggest benefits of organizing around the customer is that "we were all now in it together to win . . . and all the [traditional] functional lines will continue to get blurred. Some people are threatened by this, but I think it's very exciting. I sit in some team meetings where I don't know who's from Marketing, which is as it should be." As you would expect, P&G has set up rewards, metrics, and measures that hold executives jointly accountable for consistently delivering on customer needs.

Stengel helped to make it clear that P&G works for the customer and must serve that customer as if she were their boss. The Zappos and P&G examples in effect disregard traditional organizational lines and hierarchy and showcase the opportunity for a much more effective and profitable way to go to market—one in which the customer becomes the center of the organizational universe, with Visionary Marketers having to lead the way.

A recent study by McKinsey, *Creating Organizational Transformations*, corroborates the P&G example by noting three success factors that generally occur when companies go through a successful organizational transformation. First, clear, aspirational goals and objectives are set for the company—goals that stretch the organization in a new direction—as reflected in the P&G example in which Lafley described "putting the customer in the center of everything we do." The second factor is engaging the entire company in the transformation—the same as in Stengel's discussion about "blurring functional lines" at P&G. Third, CEO involvement and leadership are mandatory.

Clarity in Positioning

Another successful transformational approach is to lead the organization to be more customer centered by having internal and external clarity of what the organization's positioning is and, importantly, is not. In a sense, the companies that find ways to create memorable and lasting experiences with their customers are generally the ones that do the best job in galvanizing their employees to most naturally operate in a customer-centric manner. This was true fifty years ago and will be true fifty years from now. Clarity in mission, purpose, and positioning and distinct reasons to believe help every employee, from the Foreman to the CFO, understand clearly what business they are in and what role they are supposed to play.

Some companies have an easier time than others in managing in a customer-centric manner, primarily because they have already worked tirelessly to be crystal clear in what they stand for: Apple, which makes computers, but whose real business is delivering simplicity and creativity; Whole Foods, which is a grocery chain, but whose real business is delivering wellness in everyday ways; Target, which is a mass retailer, but whose real business is offering products with democratic design; Disney, which is an entertainment conglomerate, but whose real business is magic and making dreams come true; and Walmart, which is a mass retailer, but whose real business is helping consumers live a better life.

Each of these companies highlights a promise that inspires, galvanizes, and induces the company to think and organize in ways that support their positioning. Each clarifies what fits the brand and forestalls turf battles by clarifying and articulating a particular customer benefit as its central goal. To get a practical sense of this, imagine a consumer products company (say, Red Bull) trying to pitch a new beverage offering to merchants at Whole Foods that does not promote wellness; or imagine a media company (say, Weinstein Brothers) pitching a new entertainment offering to Disney that doesn't stand for magic; or think of the countless partners-in-waiting trying to pitch new accessories to Apple that do not clear the simplicity and creativity hurdles that Apple sets up in its positioning.

To this point, Target does not need to transform itself and its organization to become more customer-centric, as its clarity in positioning (offering products with democratic design) does a lot of the heavy lifting for them, but it does need to continue to energize its in-market point of view to keep its positioning fresh. A recent *Fortune* cover story by Jennifer Reingold says that Target CEO Gregg Steinhafel, his predecessor, Robert Ulrich, and Visionary Marketer Michael Francis believe that ideas, inspiration, and change come from every pocket of the company and the globe, all in service of keeping Target both fresh and relevant. As a result these three men, along with other key Target executives, have built an infectiously customer-centered environment and culture, one with minimal turnover and throngs of loyal advocates.

Leadership, inspiration, and clarity, starting from the top and working their way down, help to make transformations a lot smoother and, ideally, a way of life, but may not be enough for all companies to shift. Sometimes an economic case is required to seal the transformation.

A Bottom-Up Transformation Approach: Making a Business Case to Relentlessly Focus on the Customer

Not everyone has an inspirational leader at the top to drive the type of transformation discussed throughout this book, and not every company has an elegant in-market point of view, like Target does, to help guide core strategic decisions and important organizational shifts. In addition, not every Board or executive team member is swayed by inspiration alone (nor should they be); most need a fact-based business case to help them better understand why an internal customer-centric change is needed.

This is the challenge Dennis Cary at United Airlines faced a few years ago as the airline emerged from Chapter 11 with a more robust business model and a more efficient business operation. Cary had to prove to the board and his peers that there was one more step to take—one in which the airline could compete in a way that was unheard of for a legacy airline, with the customer at the center of the universe and the hero of the United story. Cary knew that he was playing to a tough audience, as airlines have historically been run solely to meet the numbers, not to meet nuanced customer needs. However, he also knew that all customers are not created equal: some are high touch and high mileage, paying for more and expecting more, while others shop for the cheapest fare online and consequently don't come with a lot of margin attached to them. Both types of customers (and all of those in between) are critical for an airline's success. While airlines need customers to fill every seat on a plane, not all customers are foundational to how a company builds its strategy.

To this point, Cary intuitively knew that if he could show how increasing the focus on invested high fliers (representing around 3% of all fliers)—those who fly a lot, spend a lot, change their tickets a lot, and are loyal to loyalty programs—then the airline could probably garner a disproportionate share of margin, possibly more than focusing on the other 97% of fliers. So Cary and his team went on a journey to build a robust, fact-based business case demonstrating that by just getting a small percentage of invested high fliers who fly United only a few times annually to choose to fly United as their carrier of choice most often, their chances of meeting their business and growth goals would be higher than almost any other strategy they could dream up.

Cary and his functional peers went on to build a customer-focused strategy that had the airline focus all fifty thousand employees on the things that invested high fliers wanted the most: to be relaxed, respected, and rewarded by their airline of choice. They jointly developed new programs, upgraded customer service, reevaluated everything from how airport lobbies are laid out to how benefits are delivered in the loyalty program, all as part of a continuous stream of innovations designed to keep this group of fliers motivated to stay with United over the long haul.

In designing this customer-centered strategy, not once did Cary suggest that new advertising was needed, as United had close to 100% awareness. But he and other leaders at United openly and gladly traded off budget earmarked for Marketing to implement more training, drive massive international upgrades, and develop exclusive programs, such as the Global Services check-in lounge at Chicago's O'Hare Airport, that only invested high fliers could get access to.

A reorganization did eventually take place at United, born out of necessity as well as opportunity. But a marketing-led transformation occurred at the same time. A Customer Experience group was formed, currently reporting up to Cary in his Chief Customer Officer role, to move the dial with target customers. This group works hand in hand with Operations to manage and support innovations crucial to what target customers were seeking. By combining Marketing and Customer Experience, United is able to more holistically deliver products and services that its customers value, as well as continuously seek new ways to organize around and, ultimately, delight the customer.

Cary and United worked their way from a bottom-up, business-case-driven approach to induce a customer-oriented transformation. Over the long haul, this transformation will help United to continue to weather oil price and economic fluctuations, and other storms, better than other legacy airlines because the company is built to drive loyalty with those customers who will most likely continue to fly regardless of the global, macroeconomic environment, and they will most likely continue to fly United.

The most successful transformations will generally involve some combination of inspiration and business case development to win over the hearts and minds of executives, rank-and-file employees, and ultimately customers.

Sean Burke used more than his vision and inspiration alone to convince GE to buy into his new customer-centric, go-to-market approach. Burke combined vision, inspiration, and a reason to believe with an airtight business case to sell his Growth Board on why GE Healthcare should embrace the new strategy he was recommending to fulfill its longer-term growth aspirations.

Like other Visionary Marketers, Burke helped clearly articulate what was on versus off strategy, what should be on to-do lists and what should come off, and why every business unit, geography, and functional area had to come together to bring this new strategy to life. To succeed from day one, Burke knew he must collaborate with representatives from every part of the business to develop and ultimately bring this strategy to life. He didn't want to have to sell this new strategy, which was totally centered around customer needs and expectations; he wanted it to be adopted. Thus, he created a leadership council early on (with few marketers on it) whose mission was to solve all sticky go-to-market issues. With global representation, this council became the group that pitched the final new strategy recommendations to the Board for approval, with Burke being only one of its many organizational supporters—just as he planned from the start.

Employees across GE Healthcare are aligned with this new vision and are transforming and permanently shifting how they go to market to win. Customers are now experiencing GE Healthcare differently from the way they experience key competitors, such as

Siemens, Phillips, and Toshiba. Customers see GE as having organized itself around the customer instead of organizing around the product, which had been standard practice for years.

Visionary Marketers' Additional Transformational Igniters

By this point, I hope you're inspired by Burke, Cary, Hsieh, and others, but perhaps you are still unsure about how to start. You are essentially ready to inspire, become more influential, collaborate with your peers, and engage the entire organization on a customer-centered, organizational transformation. But the task seems almost overwhelming. Here are some ways to make it less so.

Embrace Small Wins on Your Way to Making Big Changes

In Chapter One, when the hallmarks of successful Visionary Marketers were discussed, the concept of embracing small victories and trying not to be seduced into activating big-bang, game-changing shifts all at once was discussed. Not only is it risky to try to make any of these shifts happen too fast, it is also not pragmatic.

Although small wins may not be glamorous, they help build credibility, put margin points on the board, and provide the experience required to take on increased strategic challenges, collaboration, and coalition building, all from a position of strength. Brian Swette, former Chairman of Burger King and former Marketing Head at both Frito-Lay and eBay, says:

> I always think that a lot of people come in and try to pitch a broader role or try to talk someone into a new strategic mandate, but I think that is the wrong way to do it. If you want to do something, then take the action to do it and create small and immediate successes that will give you the track record and credibility to do more.

Even if it is a bigger strategic bet you are trying to make, always opt for piloting your idea, program, or strategy in the field, pulling in co-conspirators along the way. Sometimes this is making a virtue out of a necessity. Becky Saeger, CMO of Charles Schwab, was forced to start small because she operated a smaller budget than most other marketers:

> Our mandate was to cut expenses and, as such, I went into the year with a really small budget. We decided to go into only three markets and do it right, and we did! But we did so with a sophisticated test and control mind-set, collaborating with the field daily. It worked. It was about integrated marketing, collaborating and coordinating with the field, and proving out a concept before we took it out on a broader platform.

As Saeger learned, it is important to get some in-market results and impact before you make the corporatewide argument. "Start small, spend less, and learn a lot" should be your mantra as you think about deploying strategic ideas. This was also discussed in the Fourth Shift.

Build Cross-Functional Coalitions

As has been highlighted throughout this chapter and the rest of the book, collaboration and alliances built early on will help ease your way into richer strategic dialogues at business unit and functional levels and allow you to transform your organization over time to operate in a more customer-centered manner. The stories of GE, Schwab, and United, unfolded over quarters and years, not weeks or months, and each started with the Visionary Marketer celebrating small victories and aligning with other leaders in the organization to help make change happen quickly and credibly. At GE, the early coalition was with Sales. At United, it was with operations. At Burger King, it was with Operators in the field. By building these coalitions, Visionary Marketers were able to garner organizational credibility and trust (the First Shift) across key stakeholder groups and make their shifts endure over the long haul.

The right coalition-building approach may depend on where the Visionary Marketer sits on the P&L ownership spectrum. On the left end of the spectrum, Visionary Marketers operate from a highly accountable, P&L ownership position—responsible for driving top- and bottom-line results, in addition to their marketing responsibilities. On the right end of the spectrum, Visionary Marketers operate with a P&L mind-set, day in and day out, but do not actually control an income statement. With P&L ownership, coalition building comes more naturally through the built-in, ongoing forums for executive engagement that focus on top- and bottom-line results. Without ownership but with a P&L mind-set, executive engagement most likely needs to be created and forums established to allow more customer-centric, growth-oriented dialogue. Let's discuss the successful approaches leveraged with both scenarios.

Coalition Building, Starting with P&L Ownership and Accountability

Visionary Marketers who have direct P&L responsibility automatically have a seat at the table, have clear financial goals and targets, and have the added benefit of being extraordinary marketers. They already are naturally engaged in a variety of dialogues with functional and business unit heads on topics within and outside marketing's traditional domain. They have a natural forum to talk about the merits of managing from a customer perspective, tied to what the customer is saying about how the company should or should not go to market, all while focusing on their own top- and bottom-line numbers.

The advantage that Visionary Marketers get from P&L accountability is that it puts them in ongoing dialogues with other company leaders about the company's top- and bottom-line performance; this in turn gives them a clear and credible launching pad and forum for leading the organization to shift the organization around the customer. Also, they can use their pragmatic experience, examples, and data to address claims related to business and marketing agendas. These Visionary Marketers start in the trenches, building coalitions, developing ongoing alliances with their peers, and earning respect for their points of view.

The disadvantage of P&L ownership is that owners may not be seen as objective, clear, or credible when they argue for organizational shifts, especially if they appear to be land-grabbing for more marketing power or advancing their own separate P&L interests. This was the case with a high-tech CMO we know well, who owned both the marketing agenda and the E-business P&L. This CMO thought that if his E-business/Marketing organization owned the CRM system, he would be in the best position to ensure that it would be most effective in deploying comprehensive information to the sales force. Unfortunately, this was perceived by Sales as a way for Marketing to tell Sales how to do their business and to argue that this CMO's e-business was more efficient and successful than traditional selling, which was owned by the head of sales. Although there are obviously much deeper problems in an organization such as this, the example demonstrates that Visionary Marketers need to ensure that their ideas are perceived as being objective and always in the best interests of the organization.

Coalition Building Starting with a P&L Mind-Set, But Not P&L Ownership

When Visionary Marketers do not have direct P&L responsibility but do operate with a P&L mind-set and have earned credibility, they will have a seat at the table by virtue of being both extraordinary marketers and growth enablers. These Visionary Marketers are engaged in a variety of dialogues with functional and business unit heads on topics within and outside marketing's domain. Although they may not directly own a P&L, hitting the numbers every month is as critical to them as is running the P&L itself. The reality, though, for these Visionary Marketers is that they do not have as many of those built-in and natural forums for regular conversations about the growth agenda and what is best for the customer as their P&L-owning counterparts. They also may not consistently have the CEO's ear regarding trade-offs that can help propel the organization.

Coalition Building Through Expanding the Visionary Marketer Sphere of Influence

Another coalition-building approach is for Visionary Marketers to take on more critical customer touch point responsibilities. When veteran marketer Tom O'Toole was at Hyatt, he did just this when, after having responsibility for Marketing for five years, he also took responsibility for Information Technology in 2000. Although Marketing and the customer were truly his passion, he knew that in order to help drive the guest experience at Hyatt—short of actually operating one of Hyatt's hotels—he had to help lead critical touch points that corporate could control in the guest experience. For Hyatt and O'Toole, this included owning the transactional database, the loyalty program, and the online experience, from bookings, to the loyalty program, to Hyatt's new social network, *yatt'it*. By owning both Marketing and Information Technology, O'Toole became part of virtually every C-suite conversation tied to growth and the customer and was in coalition-building mode every day as part of his operational success.

The Evolution of Brand Councils to Growth Councils for Organizational Transformations

Another way to build coalitions is by activating governing bodies to help drive the growth agenda. While there may already be meetings in place that are led by the CEO and are called weekly executive team meetings or check-ins, a different type of meeting or coalition-building vehicle is needed—one that has *growth* in its title.

Over the years, many companies have successfully implemented global or executive brand councils, as suggested in my previous book, coauthored with Michael Dunn, *Building the Brand-Driven Business*. Back in 2002, when this concept was introduced, the purpose behind these councils was for marketers to have a higher-level forum in which they could lead brand-centered discussions—with the hope that they would ultimately lead to growth-oriented discussions (thus the subtitle of the book, *Operationalizing Your Brand to Drive Profitable Growth*). Back then, the executive brand council provided a forum for marketers to lead discussions around the power of brand and how companies could more effectively build their brands.

Many companies, such as Visa and AT&T, launched these councils by starting with dialogues similar to the one Randy Clouser had when he took on the CMO position at Zurich Financial (see case study). Many of these dialogues covered brand-building basics, such as moving to fewer, stronger brands; driving toward one common look and feel for the brand on a global basis; and building a global repository and set of guidelines for the brand. Some of these discussions were more strategic, while others were more tactical. Each resulted in collaborative dialogues that started to take place across the organization—dialogues that probably would not have gotten the attention they did without a more structured forum.

Consider Ann Ness's experience at Cargill. When she and the leadership team led Cargill on a brand- and customer-led journey a few years back, she realized that she was up against a few challenges:

> In the late 1990s, a new business strategy was articulated that Cargill would move beyond trading and low-cost processing to focusing on the customer and becoming the global leader in nourishing people. The business leaders of the organization developing this strategy recognized that the voice of the customer was not well understood, nor was it clear what the Cargill brand stood for in the minds of Cargill stakeholders—from farmers to the government to food manufacturers.

Describing Marketing's role, she says:

> While Marketing was slower to find a place at the table, as this was new to the organization, it became clear that we were going to have to address issues around voice of the customer and brand building. There was great intuitive pride in the 145-year-old organization, but we had put little discipline in place around the brand, and we did not have a developed understanding of the role of Marketing. Thus, the decision to build a stronger Cargill brand ultimately resulted in a new way for us to go to market, and we began the development of a stronger marketing function.

The decision led Cargill to form the Brand Council whose objective, set early on by Ness and Cargill's top executives, was to champion the Cargill brand and strategically guide its value enhancement on a global level. The leaders on the Brand Council were desirous of having a voice in all brand-related issues, directing the evolution of a branded culture, setting brand-based performance metrics, and leveraging the brand to help drive the aggressive growth agenda Cargill had established. Although the formal name of Brand Council has lived on at Cargill, the council's purpose has transitioned over time to become a much more robust forum to talk about growth.

In many respects, the transition into a growth council from a brand council represents an evolutionary strategy (instead of a new or divergent strategy). The growth council's agenda items may include topics as diverse as these, many of which are by-products of the twelve strategic growth topics discussed in Chapter One, and reflected in the Zurich Financial case study which follows:

- Tracking performance against growth agenda, strategy, segments, and targets

- Increasing brand (and thus business) relevance, reputation, and impact
- Leveraging best practices throughout the organization, across business units and functions
- Seeking out cross-collaboration and cross-selling opportunities
- Engaging the broader organization against the broader growth and brand agenda
- Upholding the brand positioning, identity, persona, and customer experience
- Driving out new product efforts, in a pervasive way
- Improving the broader return on marketing and selling investments
- Establishing and adhering to brand and performance metrics that matter

---

Zurich Financial: Living the Fifth Shift

Randy Clouser, current Chief Operating Officer, Head of the Growth Office, and former CMO for Zurich Financial, describes Zurich's customer-led growth journey:

> To drive the growth agenda, our CEO created the Growth Council. The Growth Council is a group of senior executives from each of the businesses that embody the growth mind-set and represent the key functional heads—Marketing, IT, HR, Underwriting, as well as the business units. With my background as CMO, I was asked to set the Growth Council agenda and lead discussions around growth and top-line revenue generation. As the leader, I asked all executives on the council to check their organizational and functional hats at the door. Growth is not

> a function; it is multidisciplinary mind-set. There was a whole mind-set change that needed to happen at Zurich, and we were determined to make that happen.

To get to this point where he could credibly launch a Growth Council, Clouser had to take Zurich Financial on a journey, which started when he became CMO in 2004. He recalls:

> I was appointed as CMO to coordinate and synthesize all the marketing functions in the separate companies and business divisions. We essentially had sixty variable brands that were massively underleveraged, and as part of CEO James J. Schiro's broader directive to operationally transform Zurich, we needed to migrate to a single brand and a centralized marketing division. This was a big change, and it was the first signal to the marketplace, and our employees, that we were becoming much more externally focused and customer-centric. We had strong singular brands but never truly a global, unified brand. I spent two years helping us to migrate to a single, more powerful global brand. That was my assignment.

The CMO role, Clouser remembers,

> gave me a broad understanding of the businesses, products, and opportunities and allowed me to see the business holistically. You need that vision to be able to lead growth. In addition, from the marketing and branding role, I had a richer understanding of the customer's needs and insights into what we could do better to drive the company's overall growth performance. I believed that you didn't necessarily need to be inside the individual business operations to help stretch the thinking of the business division leaders around customers, products and distribution channels. One of your primary goals as CMO is to bring about a different perspective that complements the growth agenda. During these two years, a lot of change occurred at Zurich, and I was able to

> build many bridges and alliances that helped me successfully transition into my current role.

Now, in his capacity as Chief Operating Officer and Head of the Growth Office, Clouser states,

> We have moved to an organization that has a holistic and disciplined external focus. We are more customer-centric then ever before, and this gave me license to create the Growth Office (and, thus, the Growth Council) to get more effective in our core competencies and help dramatically drive the business forward. We have connected and embedded a growth perspective in all management processes and are now down to execution and building out in-market growth streams. These growth streams are well organized, institutionalized across the organization, and are being measured and tracked. These proof points are fundamental in making this structure work in our businesses. Today, there is a different mind-set around growth at Zurich. It took the entire organization to come together and understand the opportunity to put Zurich on a trajectory to drive profitable growth.

Clouser believes the skill sets required to make an organizational transformation occur, like the one just described at Zurich, are not unlike the ones described earlier in this chapter and throughout *The Shift.* He believes that a transformational leader

> has to have a high degree of credibility and a broad understanding of the organization. They must be multidisciplinary and know how all the pieces of the business fit together. They have to have leadership skills and use these skills to become an influential leader because you don't have direct reporting relationships with many of the other leaders required to drive the growth agenda. Therefore, you need to have great persuasion and influencing abilities in getting all leaders to come to the table to talk about growth. You need to engage all leaders in dialogues in which they are talking about growth, across the entire organization, and you

> need to build an environment in which leaders who are good at growth can help other leaders who need it. And, importantly, transformational leaders have to have a solid relationship with the CEO, based on mutual respect and credibility as well as a strong track record.

Good advice from a Visionary Marketer who has lived through a successful customer-driven, growth-led, collaboration-influenced organizational transformation.

Organizational Transformation: Corporate Versus Business Unit, Centralized Versus Decentralized

What happens in a decentralized organization, in which, for example, marketing and growth discussions are happening at the business unit P&L level but you are in corporate? Or suppose your organization is centralized, but because of your global reach, by default, your company needs to go to market in a decentralized way.

The reality is that most organizations today operate in a hybrid model, which can bring the best of corporate to the business units and the best of each geography to other geographies around the globe. American Express, BP, and HP are great examples of the blended approach. These companies recognize that when they look at the broad spectrum of the growth agenda—research, segmentation, selling approaches, relevant innovations, and differing competitive sets—the company cannot have just one set of standards and approaches that apply unilaterally across all offerings, segments, and business units. Often a Global Growth Council is established within these organizations to help navigate through larger, more strategic issues that need full BU and geographic participation. Here is a quick review of the principles that separate or differentiate centralized from decentralized firms as well as the pragmatic aspects of the blended approach for Visionary Marketer to think about:

	Centralized Firms	**Decentralized Firms**	**Blended**
Marketing ownership	The corporate center directs marketing activities.	Business unit or regional marketing groups operate independently.	Business unit or regional marketing groups are autonomous but have an indirect report to the corporate center.
Marketing coordination	Marketing activities are interdependent, with multiple marketing-related functions, such as research, graphic design, and promotions, all reporting to the center.	Marketing operates minimally with other functions or business units and is perceived as a separate organization, often providing value-added services and points of view to the rest of the organization.	Marketing activities are coordinated with similar functions like Sales but minimally with others.
Team organization	Teams are organized around key customers or customer segments.	Teams are organized around product categories or brands.	Teams are organized around products and customers (either separately or combined).

Beth Comstock, CMO of GE, lives in such a blended world. She runs global brand, advertising, and growth councils, but she also recognizes the realities and practicalities of running a global $200 billion enterprise. She believes that for Visionary Marketing to work at GE from an organizational perspective, Marketing has to be a growth catalyst (speeding things up and pulling different functions and pieces together), in addition to helping with overall market development. She relies on the business units and the geographies to run point on what is best for their individual businesses and global operations, but actively distributes global standards and best practices for all to leverage, while chairing and being part of several global councils that require across-the-board voices and votes.

As you would expect of one with her purview, Comstock vigilantly makes sure that the voice of the customer is front and center in every discussion she has about corporate and business unit marketing. She strongly believes that the customer cuts through all organizational walls and barriers. And when a Visionary Marketer leads with the voice of the customer, as Cargill's Ann Ness said, "everyone sits up and pays attention."

We're All in This Together

Remember some of the guiding principles that make any organizational transformation work and stick for the long term. Because they are fundamental for real change to occur, they are worth repeating:

- Align the goals and objectives of functional and geographical heads to the goals of the company. Once there is total alignment between goals, objectives, and strategies with execution, results, and metrics, everyone will get on the same page.
- For long-term success, the CEO must be a proponent of the transformation. Having the CEO co-sponsor or lead

it with the Visionary Marketer helps to make *The Shift* happen.

- Building a transformational business case, road map, and story to tell will help in getting the entire organization, especially executive peers, to see the tangible and intangible rationale behind making *The Shift*. Without this rationale, the odds of another program du jour fall-out are high.
- The important mind-set shift is to recognize that everyone reports to the customer. It helps to eradicate functional silos and turf battles, perpetuate an outside-in point of view, and motivate the troops to see the real reason to go to this type of transformation—actually the only reason—to better serve the customer.

So, What Do I Do on Monday Morning?

Here are things to consider in your organization as you think about shifting from an organizational focus to a relentless customer focus:

1. Assess where you and your company are in terms of ability, desire, and openness to address the idea of taking a fresh look at how your organization is or is not set up to win with customers.
2. Get a clear understanding of how all functional areas relate back to the customer and map out how each function helps to either drive and close or inhibit the sale.
3. Clearly understand business priorities and how a more customer-centric orientation helps drive those priorities.
4. Determine if your organization will benefit most by having a top-down-driven mandate of why organizing around the

customer makes sense (as P&G does), or more of a bottom-up business economic case (as at United Airlines), or both (as at GE Healthcare). Regardless of which approach (it will most likely be a combination), set up a team with cross-functional representation to help initiate the process.

5. Begin to create alliances and coalitions with groups that directly or indirectly touch the customer. Focus on those that will help you get to the quickest wins, that garner trust and credibility, or that may be the most difficult to win over (such as Finance).
6. Within these alliances and coalitions, seek out small wins and proof points, tied to coming together to win the battle for the customer.
7. Make sure all initiatives you take on are still housed underneath the overall strategic umbrella of what the organization is trying to accomplish over the next three to five years.
8. Consider initiating a Growth Council, which should be a natural outcome for the Visionary Marketer to charter if the First Shift has been successfully made. Make sure traditional marketing agenda items are housed underneath strategic, growth-oriented imperatives, not as marketing tactic updates.
9. Appreciate nuances tied to centralized versus decentralized and single business versus multiple or diverse businesses and multiple geographies. Be transparent in how these affect the approach your organization takes in starting to organize around the customer.
10. Get going. Start small, and recognize that you are on a customer-focused journey. Pick a geography, a line of business, or a functional area, and start organizing for greater impact in ways in which your customer would expect you to be organized—around how they want to do business with you.

AFTERWORD

Shifting Is Not Easy

Making *The Shift* is a major statement, a necessity, a symbol, and a transformation—all at the same time. There is as much importance in the five shifts for marketers as there are for those companies and their executive teams looking for new and better ways to reach their growth aspirations. If you buy into the premise that organic growth will continue to be a challenge for executives committed to reaching their stated growth goals, especially as sustained economic pressures continue to force companies to make much smarter investment trade-off decisions, then the battle for the customer will never be as tough as it will be over the next decade.

At the time this book is being written, the global economic climate is as tough to operate, compete, and thrive in as at any other time in at least a generation. The pressures that companies are experiencing are suffocating for most, and the trickle-down and trickle-up effect of the pullback is felt in every pocket of business. This deeply affects how marketers are operating today and how they will need to shift to help their company survive and, arguably, their position survive, especially if the marketer as tactician is the operating norm. Nonetheless, the challenges will continue.

Price/value equations will be called into question. The ability to directly reach your target customer will become more elusive. Your ability to control the message, and thus the relationship, will become even more slippery, and the somewhat desperate need for increased depths of customer loyalty will never be greater. Going forward, every marketing dollar spent will be microscopically judged internally, just as every move you make in the marketplace will be judged (sometimes harshly) through an external lens. Through all of this, Marketing, and marketers in general, will continue to be challenged to prove their own ROI and worth to their respective companies.

To this point, a number of the executives interviewed for this book now have new titles, both within and outside the company they represented when originally interviewed. I would fully expect that half of the executives interviewed for *The Shift* will be in different positions within a year of this book's publication. In addition, a number of companies featured in this book have gone through major reorganizations since profiled, and every company has been subjected to severe external economic conditions—some with better results than others. No one has the luxury of remaining complacent.

The transformation highlighted in this book's title, and the shifts encompassed within, are not going to cure all ills confronting today's marketers, especially if their respective organizations do not fully embrace the power of marketing. These shifts are meant to start to change the dialogue, recalibrate the expectations for Marketing, and shift internal power bases in fundamentally game-changing ways. Once and for all, the idea that marketing is just discretionary spend, housed in a corporate function, not responsible for true demand generation, will be eradicated from the dialogue. *The Shift* is not just about a repositioning of marketing. At its core, it is meant to give your organization a considerable edge over the competition.

So what does *shifting* really mean for marketers, their respective companies, and their customers?

For marketers, it fundamentally means they are given the opportunity to rebrand the marketing role and function, as well as their overall positioning within their company, from being *just* a sales enabler to being a value driver across the entire enterprise. For the company, embraced to its fullest extent, making *The Shift* means that CEOs and boards will have an organic growth driver that they potentially did not have in their arsenal in the past. The company will now have a much greater depth of customer insight, meaningful new revenue and margin streams, and a return on all marketing and sales dollars that should go well beyond traditional norms.

Finally, for the customer, it means the opportunity to build a relationship with the company that is mutually beneficial to both the company and the customer. It means the company is communicating with customers in ways that are relevant to their lives, and not just to the company. It means new offerings will be developed that are, in effect, a by-product of customers' stated needs, wants, and desires, in a codeveloped way. And it means that customers will be supported by the company, and its brand, in an unintrusive yet relationship-oriented manner, with the hope that this will result in depths of customer loyalty and stickiness that neither the customer nor the company has experienced before.

Let's briefly summarize what marketers should hope to accomplish after each of the five shifts are successfully made.

The First Shift: From Creating Marketing Strategies to Driving Business Impact. In this First Shift, marketers will try to alter the dialogue and engage and lead discussions around the future growth goals and aspirations for the organization. The hope is that they will operate in an organizational construct that supports the

Visionary Marketer, and not the Tactician Marketer, which will lead to discussions around what segments to target, what white spaces need to be filled, how best to galvanize the internal and external stakeholder base, and what strategy will ultimately support the five-year growth gap. Charles Schwab, GE, Walmart, and Burger King were among those held up as great examples of those companies that live the first shift.

The Second Shift: From Controlling the Message to Galvanizing Your Network. In this shift, Visionary Marketers will, in effect, cede control of their brand to their customers, recognizing that the real end game will be getting the sale and not just about the command and control of top of the funnel awareness building. Thriving in the Network Era will entail understanding the myriad of touch points that directly and indirectly influence the sale and allow you to consciously make informed, on-strategy choices as to which touch points you will try to influence and which you will allow the market to influence for you. This shift is about establishing and building deeper relationships in more meaningful and relevant ways to ultimately drive customer stickiness. Apple, Nike, Dell, and Zappos were among those held up as great examples of companies that live the Second Shift.

The Third Shift: From Incremental Improvements to Pervasive Innovation. In this shift, Visionary Marketers will help their organizations see innovation as a way of life and an engine for growth and relevance that most companies have not experienced before. This shift helps to dispel the notion that innovation is an event that occurs in a pipeline-oriented manner; it needs to happen every day and in every pocket of the organization. Like the Second Shift, pervasive innovation heavily relies on the customer's being deeply intertwined in all innovation efforts. Co-creation, codevelopment and embracing a not-invented-here approach are all critical for the Third Shift to take hold. P&G, Boeing, Adobe, and Best Buy were among those offered as outstanding examples of companies that live the Third Shift.

The Fourth Shift: From Managing Marketing Investments to Driving Marketing Excellence. In the Fourth Shift, Visionary Marketers will help their organizations recognize that the great advances that organizations have made in marketing mix modeling and overall marketing effectiveness efforts are just the tip of the iceberg. Tomorrow, the discussion about how best to leverage marketing investment has to be morphed into how best to use customer acquisition dollars across all of Kotler's 4 P's. In effect, Visionary Marketers need to be leading the charge in terms of how to best make smart trade-off decisions across all elements of Big M marketing tied to winning the customer's business, regardless of whether the budget dollars are housed within a traditional marketing budget. UnitedHealthcare, Staples, Nationwide, and Hyatt were among those held up as great examples of those companies that live the Fourth Shift.

The Fifth Shift: From an Operational Focus to a Relentless Customer Focus. In this Fifth Shift, Visionary Marketers will help their organizations truly understand why breaking down traditional organizational norms and functional barriers is critical to building a tighter bond with customers. Marketing influence is the currency here, and deepening levels of loyalty is the pay-off to organizing around the customer. Zurich Financial, DKSH, GE Healthcare, and United Airlines were among those held up as great examples of those companies that live the Fifth Shift.

For marketers to succeed at these five shifts, the assumption is that they have successfully migrated from being Tactician Marketers to Visionary Marketers. It means that they have established a dialogue with the executive team and the board that is strategic in nature but pragmatic in execution. It means that they have changed their profile and perception from being seen solely as a cost center to a powerful revenue (and margin) driver. And finally, these marketers have become partners with their CEOs, helping to articulate and drive their company's growth agenda from here on in. Quite a shift, indeed!

Good luck as you start *The Shift* within your own company.

BIBLIOGRAPHY

Bernstein, F. "Montreal: Aloft Montreal Airport." Aug. 2008. http://travel.nytimes.com/2008/08/17/travel.

Bloom, J. "The Truth Is: Consumers Trust Fellow Buyers Before Marketers." Feb. 2006. http://findarticles.com/p/articles/mi_hb6398/is_200602/ai_n25576930.

Collier, M. "Dell: A Social Media Rags-to-Riches Story." Oct. 2007. http://moblogsmoproblems.blogspot.com/2007/10/dell-social-media-rags-to-riches-story.html.

Commander, C., Wilson, M., and Stevenson, J. *The Evolved* CMO. Forrester Research and Heidrick & Struggles, 2007.

Creating Organizational Transformations: McKinsey Global Survey Results. McKinsey & Company, 2008.

Cummings, J. "Obama, the Billion-Dollar Man." Dec. 2008. http://www.nytimes.com.

Davis, S. *Brand Asset Management: Driving Profitable Growth Through Your Brands*. San Francisco: Jossey-Bass, 2000.

Dunn, M., and Davis, S. *Building the Brand-Driven Business: Operationalize Your Brand to Drive Profitable Growth*. San Francisco: Jossey-Bass, 2002.

Dunn, M., and Halsall, C. *The Marketing Accountability Imperative*. San Francisco: Jossey-Bass, 2009.

Fass, H. "Innovate in a Recession? Yes It Can Be Done: If Anything, the Economic Downturn Creates a Unique Opportunity for Marketers." Feb. 2008. http://adage.com/abstract.php?article_id=125242.

Field, P. "What Obama Can Teach You About Millennial Marketing." *Advertising Age*, August 2008.

Fisher, A. "Ideas Made Here." June 2007. http://money.cnn.com/magazines/fortune/fortune_archive.

Fortt, J. "Michael Dell 'Friends' His Customers." Sept. 2008. http://money.cnn.com/2008/09/03/technology/fortt_dell.fortune.

"'Gamma Women' 55 Million Strong, to Define New Marketing Model." Sept. 2008. http://www.marketingcharts.com/interactive/gamma-women-55-million-strong-to-define-new-marketing-model-5925.

Hannon, K. "Marketers Get to Us in More Ways." Aug. 2008. http://www.usatoday.com/money/books/reviews.

Holmes, S. "Nike, Google Kick Off Social-Networking Site." Mar. 2006. http://www.businessweek.com/technology/content.

How Companies Approach Innovation: A McKinsey Global Survey. McKinsey, 2007.

"IBM Invests $100 Million in Collaborative Innovation Ideas." Nov. 2006. http://www-03.ibm.com/press/us/en/pressrelease/20605.wss.

Jarvis, M. Presentation at the Fifth Annual Merkle DbM Executive Summit, Austin, Tex., May 2008.

Johnson, B. "Survey Finds CFOs Skeptical of Their Own Firms' ROI Claims." July 2008. http://adage.com/abstract.php?article_id=129629.

Johnson, C. "Hurry Up, the Customer Has a Complaint." July 2008. http://www.boston.com/business/technology/articles/2008/07/07/hurry_up_the_customer_has_a_complaint/.

Kahaner, L. *Competitive Intelligence: How to Gather, Analyze, and Use Information to Move Your Business to the Top*. New York: Touchstone, 1996.

Lafley, A. G., and Charan, R. *The Game-Changer: How You Can Drive Revenue and Profit Growth with Innovation*. New York: Crown, 2008.

Landry, E., Tipping, A., and Kumar, J. *Growth Champions*. Booz Allen Hamilton and the Association of National Advertisers, 2004.

"Marketers Are More Accountable Than Ever for Business Results." Oct. 2008. http://www.saovangdatviet.org/index.php?Module=Content&Action=view&id=2396&Itemid=30.

Marketing Outlook 2008. CMO Council, 2008.

"McDonald's Supersized Gains." Aug. 2007. http://www.businessweek.com/magazine/content/07_32/b4045418.htm.

McGregor, J., and others. "The World's Most Innovative Companies." Apr. 2008. http://www.businessweek.com/magazine/content/08_17/b3981401.htm.

McGuire, D. "Nike 6.0 Goes Viral with Online Social Community on the Loop'd Network." June 2008. http://www.reuters.com/article/pressRelease.

Measuring Innovation 2008: Squandered Opportunities. Boston Consulting Group, 2008.

Mullman, J. "To Build Buzz for Its Brands, Beam's All Talk." Aug. 2007. http://adage.com/abstract.php?article_id=120089.

"My Starbucks Idea." N.d. http://mystarbucksidea.force.com.

"Nike + Community = Leadership." Apr. 2008. http://gobigalways.com/nike/.

"Nike Foundation and Buffetts Join to Invest $100 Million in Girls." May 2008. http://www.nikebiz.com/media/pr.

O'Brien, J. "Zappos Knows How to Kick It." Jan. 22, 2009. http.//money.cnn.com/2009/01/15/news/companies/zappos_best_companies_obrien.fortune/index.htm.

"OfficeMax Magic." Sept. 2008. http://hubmagazine.com/html/2008/sep_oct/officemax.html.

O'Regan, R., and von Hoffman, C. "Interview: Jim Stengel, Procter & Gamble." Sept. 2005. http://magnostic.wordpress.com/best-of-cmo/interview-jim-stengel-procter-gamble/.

Prophet's 2005 State of Marketing Survey: Driving Business Growth. Prophet, 2005.

Reingold, J. "Target's Inner Circle." Mar. 2008. http://money.cnn.com/2008/03/18/news/companies/reingold_target.fortune/.

"Robert Pollack, VP-Brand and Market Positioning, Boeing Commercial Airplanes." Oct. 2006. http://www.btobonline.com/apps/pbcs.dll.

Schultz, H. "Howard Schultz Transformation Agenda Communication #1." Jan. 2008. http://www.starbucks.com/aboutus/pressdesc.asp?id=814.

Senge, P., and others. *The Dance of Change: The Challenges to Sustaining Momentum in Learning Organizations*. New York: Doubleday, 1999.

Stetler, B. "The Facebooker Who Friended Obama." July 2008. http://www.nytimes.com.

Story, L. "The New Advertising Outlet: Your Life." Oct. 2007. http://www.nytimes.com/2007/10/14/business/media.

2006/2007 State of Marketing Study: The Effectiveness Imperative. Prophet, 2006/2007.

2008 Best Practices Study: The Making of World-Class Innovators. Prophet and Play, 2008.

Voight, J. "The New Brand Ambassadors." Dec. 2007. http://www.adweek.com/aw.

INDEX